AF661986

THE GUIDE TO HOROSCOPE INTERPRETATION

The similarities and differences charted out by astrology, to the degree they are effective, have a meaning as varying as life itself. While all Aries people are alike in their measure of conformity to the "Aries" potential, they also are different because each according to his genius is conforming in varying ways to other potentials.

The Guide to Horoscope Interpretation

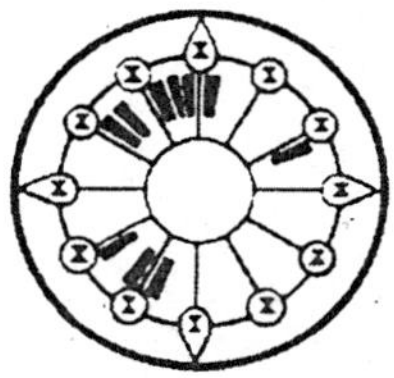

MARC EDMUND JONES

New Age Books

ISBN: 81-7822-094-6

First Indian Edition: 2003

(Published by arrangement with
Theosophical Publishing House, Illinois, USA)

Third Edition: 1982, USA

© 1941 & 1969 by Marc Edmund Jones

All rights reserved. No part of this publication may be reproduced or transmitted in any form or by any means, electronic or mechanical, including photocopying, recording, or by any information storage and retrieval system, without permission in writing from the publishers.

Published by
NEW AGE BOOKS
A-44 Naraina Phase-I
New Delhi-110 028 (INDIA)
Email: nab@vsnl.in
Website: www.newagebooksindia.com

Printed in India
at Shri Jainendra Press
A-45 Naraina Phase-I, New Delhi-110 028

contents

The horoscope is the man
because it tells what the man may be.
The measure is in the heavens
because the sky is the limit
not the limitation of human capacity.

FOREWORD

SINCE modern education outgrew the "faculty" or pigeonhole psychology, at about the turn of the century, the problem of teaching in any field, whether astrology or economics, has been to equip the student with a means for organizing his understanding, and at the same time to prevent him from tucking facts and relations away in neat little packages, under the old classical notion that a living and liquid universe can be expected to hold some static form. Nature is experienced, rather than charted. No one can ever subtract himself from the world, even momentarily, to observe its workings from the outside. Experience sorts out facets of a whole existence, and shows them separate or absolute for the instant, but this is not a revelation of realities. Rather, these aspects of experience have been abstracted from the whole according to individual desire or necessity.

Any clarification of phenomena, or classification of things and events, takes place in the human mind, and is no more than a convenience of understanding. In consequence, this text offers a technique of judgment, but not a series of patterns which can be said to have any existence outside their function as guiding factors in the process of analysis. Astrology, like any psychology, is able to predict the probabilities in a given situation because it relates experience to other experience. Experience itself is constant change, and any predictive judgment must obviously have a continual reorientation. The similarities and differences charted by astrology, to the degree they are effective, have a meaning as varying as life itself. While all

Aries people are alike in their measure of conformity to the "Aries" potential, they also are all different because each according to his own genius is conforming in varying ways to other potentials.

The division of all people into seven basic types is a purely psychological screening. The people made distinct from each other by this classification may be quite alike by some other, but this way of sorting has an effective psychological result that is hard to match in the terms of actual problems solved. These seven temperament-sets provide both the beginner and the skilled practitioner with an utterly simple point of beginning in astrological analysis. The sole danger is that this very simplicity may encourage an over-simplification, and lead to the pigeonhole thinking of the medievals. It is not important that a man is a *splash* type, but it is very vital that he make full use of his *splash* genius.

New York City, October 2, 1941.

WHAT IS A HOROSCOPE?

For those unfamiliar with the technicalities, a brief introduction may be helpful. The earth has two primary motions in the heavens, or its rotation on its axis once a day and its journey around its orbit annually. The two great circles so established are brought together to make the horoscopic wheel. Each of them is divided into twelve equal parts represented in the diagram by pie-shaped areas of indication. The ones created by the faster or daily motion are the houses, and they are commonly represented by printed lines in the horoscope. The ones similarly marked off in the earth's orbit, commonly known as the zodiac, are the familiar signs beginning with Aries and running through Pisces. Because the two great circles do not lie in the same heavenly plane, they lean away from each other and this fact permits the fundamental charting of variety in human individuality. And then the further fact that the houses are marked off in their circle from the position in the heavens of the terrestrial horizon at birth enormously increases the possibilities of horoscopic variations. Because it would be confusing to show the areas of indication of both circles by actual lines of boundary in the horoscopic wheels, astrologers note the corresponding zodiacal sign and degree at the beginning of each house from the horizon at the left and as the signs rise clockwise.

The mathematics in preparing a horoscope is most simple, but newcomers find it difficult because of many corrections that have to be made to adjust different kinds of measures to each other. Everything needed for the calculations is readily available in tabular form. As the horizontal line in the printed horoscope wheel represents the actual horizon at the place and time of birth or other event to be interpreted, the vertical line identifies at the top the midheaven or dividing point between the rising and setting motion of anything to be observed in the heavens. This midheaven is regular at any given moment of true sun time for anybody anywhere on the earth, but the corresponding horizons are almost inevitably irregular in comparison with each other because they are established on the round surface of the earth and so usually fall away from any ideal regularity. An ephemeris locates the proper midheaven and the astrologer has Tables of Houses that tell him where the horizon and other houses will be at whatever terrestrial latitude a significant occasion takes place. In the case of George Gershwin on page 57 (the most recent birth of the examples of completed horoscopic diagram) the astrologer from his ephemeris found that on September 26, 1898, the "sidereal time" or house-circle place of the midheaven on noon of that day at Greenwich in England was 12 hours and 21 minutes. The composer was born in Brooklyn where the time is approximately five hours earlier. This means a technical correction for the movement of the sun in creating noon, but it is very slight. His birth however was roughly an hour before noon, and in an hour the earth rotates an appreciable distance in the house circle. Correction for that would make the "sidereal time" of his midheaven the approximate hour earlier that has provided the astrological chart found in the book.

The second and equally simple procedure in calculating the horoscope is placing the various planets in the wheel. This involves direct proportion. If birth is so much of the day from one noon to the next, and a planet moves a certain number of zodiacal degrees in that particular day, it is easy to see how far the planet at birth has moved from noon. Exceptional factors will require adjustment, and most astrologers generally spare themselves by changing the time of birth to its equivalent at Greenwich in using the ephemeris prepared for Greenwich. Gershwin's case of 11:09 A.M. changes to approximately 4 P.M. at Greenwich. This is one-sixth of the day. Taking the sun, which almost averages an even 60 minutes daily, it would be 10′ farther than Libra 3°25′ on September 26 in the ephemeris or at Libra 3°35′ in the horoscope.

Many easily available and competent textbooks present the mathematics fully and with abundant examples.

HOW TO RECOGNIZE PLANETARY PATTERNS

Introduction

THE METHOD OF WHOLE VIEW

A HOROSCOPE is like the man it represents. It must be seen as a whole before any intelligent idea of its parts is possible. A hand may be described, and much learned about its functions. An artist can study the characteristic play of light over its curving lines. The anatomist can trace out every little muscle, nerve and capillary. However, in all these cases, the hand is a hand-in-general. It is only when hands are attached to bodies, and bodies become the abode of personality, that a hand acquires any particular importance. The mother's pat of love, the mechanic's touch of skill, reveal the hand as it takes on practical significance.

In astrology the general fact that the sun is in Aries, or any other sign, and that the moon and the other planets are likewise placed at various points around the zodiac, has a general meaning which can be put into textbooks, as the remarks upon hands in an artist's manual. But these astrological indications are of no everyday value until they are seen in the pattern of a horoscope, and applied to the whole context of a given person's life. Ultimately the interpretation of any astrological chart resolves itself into the careful analysis of each detail, but this cannot be done intelligently unless the interpreter possesses a whole-concept of the individual.

Astrology reflects the experience it patterns. Men instinctively approach their understanding of the details in experience through their conception of the whole situation, the whole person, and the whole pertinency of the moment. This is true whether the "whole" in question is observed, or taken for granted. When one man meets another on the street, he may notice a hat, suit or necktie, but unwittingly, if not otherwise, he has put that individual into a whole scheme-of-things before perceiving any particular detail. The place of meeting, the social relationship between observer and observed, together with a myriad unsuspected factors, all conspire to establish the frame of reference in which the hat, suit or necktie becomes the basis of attention. The touch of a hand, in similar fashion, may seem a simple independent fact of experience, but a background of the whole is no less essential. It might be a beggar plucking a sleeve, a friend intercepting someone who fails to see him pass in a crowd, even the accident of a person groping in the dark. The boy touches the girl, and his hand may cause her to shrink away or thrill with warmth, depending on his identity and her sense of the motive behind his gesture. Analysis that proceeds from disconnected details alone, in any walk of life, is always inadequate.

The outstanding modern development in horoscope interpretation has been the perfection of methods for recognizing the whole-factors in a chart before attempting any analysis of details. This is the technique of focal determination, i.e., the identification of "determinators of focal emphasis". The astrologers who for several generations have prepared the ground for this method have shown the significance of certain simple planetary patterns, such as the cosmic cross, the grand trine and the stellium, and also have pointed to the significant distribution of astrological qualities, such as the emphasis of quadrature and triplicity in the signs, and of corresponding elements in the houses. Exactly as all individuals can be distinguished according to their various temperaments, so all horoscopes can be classified according to the general temperament-set revealed through the focal determination. The student can begin a study of astrology by mastering the easier focal-determination types. As he grows in experience he becomes familiar with more and more unusual cases, and finally develops the skill to determine the points of whole-focus in any chart.

Because the focal determinators are very definite, both in form and implication, it is obvious that each of them will be found in only a certain percentage of horoscopes. While some may be recognized easily, at a glance, many demand a careful study of the chart, and a few require the tabulation of relations which are not evident to the eye. As a result some horoscopes may be classified instantly, whereas others reveal the native's whole pattern only after considerable analysis. Occasional cases present insuperable difficulties to all but highly skilled professionals. This has created a demand for a means by which anyone, from the beginner to the expert, can sort out all charts, with no exceptions, in some effective form of whole-view, and be able to do this at a glance.

This text meets the need with a classification which arranges all horoscopes into seven simple basic types. These seven distinctions are all-inclusive, because the method of approach makes it possible for each of the groups to shade into one or more of the others. The method is in sharp contrast with the formal classification under focal determination. The seven basic types give a clue to the nature of the entire individuality, whether they are found in the ideal case, sharply defined, or in the borderline instance where classification is possible under more than one of the types. The astrologer need not worry over the correctness of his identification when he is in doubt because, as long as he is able to see a given chart in terms of one of the types, it will unerringly reveal its whole nature to his own perspective in the lineaments of that type. He is ordering his own mind, and giving a basic direction to his own judgment.

There is no inconsistency with life here. Human beings are able to judge each other's actions accurately enough under whatever whole view each is able to establish in his estimate of the other. A selfish man may see another as selfish, and so conceive his unselfishness to be shiftlessness. A third less selfish individual, placing the second under the concept of unselfishness, may understand his generous impulses more correctly, but by the same token may consider his efforts in self-interest as fearfulness. Both the first man and the third may anticipate the characteristic reactions of the second with equal skill, and act accordingly. Their whole view is a convenience of their own judgment. It is better as it is more complete, but it can never be wholly correct in any absolute sense. Every individual, after all, must see others to some extent in terms of himself, and the greatest value of astrology is that it minimizes the distortion of judgment under this psychological fallacy. When men are seen in patterns they are found in their closest approach to their own potentiality.

The pattern-types have been developed as a means for quick and accurate preliminary classification. They are a guide to horoscope interpretation because, in the first place, they have the broadest possible orientation, and in the second, they facilitate the recognition of the focal determinators with which, under proper circumstances, the interpretation of the horoscope begins. The present text introduces and illustrates these basic pattern-types with actual examples, shows how they illuminate the focal determinators in the example charts, and indicates how the interpretation proceeds under the guidance of a whole-view established in this fashion.

The standards and practices to which the book adheres are those almost universally accepted among American and British astrologers. Judgments, as far as possible, are made from a horoscope based not only on the day, month and year of birth, but also on the exact place and time, the latter obtained to the minute by "rectification" if it is not available otherwise. The elements of the horoscope are those established by several centuries of practical use and verification.

The text is prepared so that only a minimal amount of technical knowledge will be required from the reader. There is no necessity that he learn how to "set up" or "erect" the horoscope itself, since there are example charts in astrological books everywhere, and since any number of individuals and organizations offer their services in making this "chart", "wheel", "map", or "figure" for interested non-astrologers. The reader must know the diagram form of the horoscope, but this is shown in the example cases, both in specially simplified and complete fashion. The detailed essentials he may need by way of names, symbols and other elements are outlined fully in Appendix A.

The book introduces the seven types in the first section, illustrating these in the charts of forty-nine outstanding individuals and identifying all the basic focal determinators. In the second section it proceeds to the planetary patterns, and shows how to identify the lines of human behavior as a further or more detailed guide to horoscope interpretation.

A great amount of supplementary material is given in the appendices, available for readers according to their varying needs and interests. Appendix B presents a full summary and account of focal determination. Appendix C supplies the data for the complete charts in the case of those examples given in simplified piano-key form, and also for all horoscopes to which incidental reference is made. Appendix D provides the sources of all charts, together with much special information concerning their validity and the standards adopted in checking them.

A complete topical index facilitates a comparative study of the example horoscopes, and aids the use of the text in classroom work.

CHAPTER ONE

THE SPLASH TYPE

WHAT is a planetary pattern? Obviously it is any arrangement of the planets around the zodiac that can be recognized, or identified. There are many possibilities, but the simplest of all is when the planets are distributed evenly, or splashed all the way around the circle. It is easy to see this in the horoscope, and to recognize this situation among them as "scattered". Here is a convenient point of beginning in the classification of astrological charts. Any individual with his planets rather well divided around the wheel is said to belong to the *splash* type.

An important caution must be sounded at this point. Only the ten planets are considered in the recognition of these types. Most astrologers put the dragon's head and dragon's tail in charts, as well as the Part of Fortune. These have an important significance, as the reader new to astrology may note by reference to Appendix A, but they are of no assistance in this classification of the horoscope. In astrology the planets indicate the activity of experience, or the individual's participation in a complex of interacting forces, and the astrologer therefore looks to the planets for his basic patterns.

The preliminary classification of charts into seven simple types makes no distinction among the planets themselves. It is of no consequence what particular planet occupies what particular place in the pattern, as long as the pattern itself is not destroyed. A given native has his planets scattered around the zodiac when they are fairly evenly spaced through the signs. He belongs to the *splash* type whether the sun is near the moon or not, and whether Jupiter is here or there. As a result this fundamental distinction of horoscopic types is quite independent of the house cusps. It remains an accurate and fundamental guide to horoscope interpretation even if the exact hour of birth is wrong, or is unknown, provided the date of birth is correct. Only most exceptionally will the moon's motion in twenty-four hours be sufficient to destroy the basic pattern-type, although it may often alter the focal determination. Indeed, two cases of charts where the hour is unknown, and at least one where it may well be incorrect, are included in the forty-nine examples in order to illustrate how effective the interpretation can be under unfavorable conditions.

In the witty terms of a practical American philosophy, whatever "is" makes a difference, and there is no use looking at anything except to see the difference it makes; that is, to find out what it means, what it can do, or for what it can be used. In astrology it is silly to identify anything in a chart except to find out something about the life it represents. What can the native do? What opportunity is his, by the circumstances in which he finds himself or by the skills and capabilities he has developed and made his own? The horoscope is not a map of the heavens, but a map of man as his existence makes a difference, even in the heavens. The heavens reveal the difference by the time and space factors which the man builds into the substance of his being, and the astrologer takes these differences out of the heavens through the horoscope, bringing them to bear upon the problems of everyday life. This is the simple philosophy of astrology, and the explanation of its effectiveness.

If a chart classifies under the *splash* type, it must indicate that an individual makes a "splashing difference" in life. What does this mean? At its worst it means scattered. An individual with his planets splashed out at every angle may well be like Stephen Leacock's hero, who got on his horse and "rode off in all directions". At its best, it means a capacity for a genuine universal interest, and a gift for ordering what to lesser ability might seem utter confusion. Here is the fundamental relationship, of all things to all other things, by which the universe is a consistent whole. The point can be illustrated in very familiar terms.

Warlike men tend to gravitate to a situation of conflict. Other men, finding themselves in the midst of turmoil, will tend to move into a more congenial set of circumstances on the one hand, or to become tumultuous on the other. Greedy men are inclined to seek the place where accumulation and sharp competition are found, just as adventuresome spirits will sail the seas looking for trouble. Consequently the scattered souls in life are largely to be identified in connection with scattered situations. "Scatter" is the difference which is fundamental in their nature, and in the make-up of their characteristic environment. It can be the basis of splendid achievement, since there is a place in the world for those who spread things, carry ideas and expand experience; and also the basis of bitter failure, since there is an equal place for those who waste things, lead men astray in their thinking, and actually disintegrate experience. Theirs is an unwitting and unfortunate contribution to change and reconstruction, but no less an everyday part of reality.

These seven types are therefore no indication either of success or its lack, and they give no insight into the exact potentialities which the detailed interpretation of the horoscope will provide. But they do give the general pattern of a native's self-expression, and this is an all-important guiding factor. Actually, with this alone, it is sometimes possible to give good advice, and to shape action intelligently, as will be shown through the examples.

The illustrations will have to be from cases of well-known people, and this means that the interpretation will largely be in terms of the success they have gained under the pattern, to become well-known. Failure may equally well result, but even in such an instance the individual can still turn his life into the paths of achievement. He may best do this by taking advantage of the life-pattern which the horoscope reveals. To help him do this is the single justification for the practice and study of astrology.

The *splash* type has a convenient and outstanding illustration in the horoscope of Jacob Böhme.

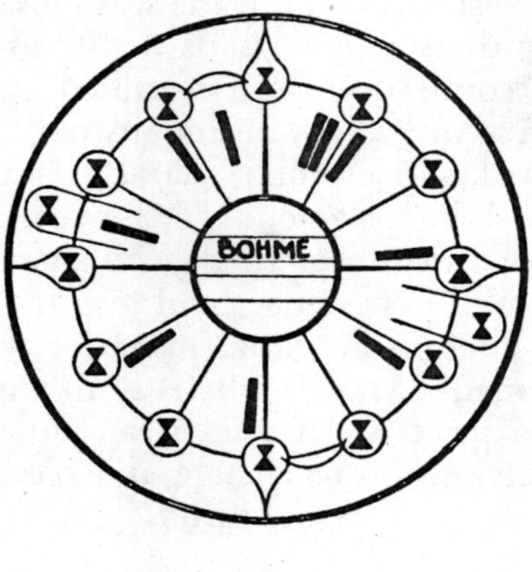

Here plain black marks are substituted for the planets and signs to reveal the *splash* type more clearly. This also dramatizes the fact that these patterns hold their general indication, irrespective of the particular places occupied by the ten planets and twelve signs, in relation to the twelve houses and to each other. The full data for Böhme's chart, as well as for the twenty other horoscopes presented in this piano-key form, is made available for the student in Appendix C.

Böhme's chart shows the ten planets fairly evenly divided, or scattered around the twelve houses. Three of the houses are empty, but no two of them next to each other. Only one contains two planets. The scattering is almost as definitely marked when the planets are taken in terms of the signs, especially when it is remembered that Mercury and Venus can never get very far away from the sun. There is an intercepted pair of signs, and these, together with the pair found on the cusps of more than one house, are differentiated by special light lines in the diagram. Böhme's planets are placed in seven of the twelve signs. In the case where two planets are in the same sign, they are more than thirteen degrees apart, or are not in conjunction. Where three planets are together in another sign, only two are in close conjunction, and the third is barely within the extreme of orb allowed for the aspect. The reader who is unfamiliar with astrological terms will find explanations of intercepted signs and orbs of aspect in Appendix A.

Jacob Böhme was born in poverty, apprenticed to a shoemaker at an early age, and held by circumstances to a very simple pattern of personal life. He received no formal instruction at all, and knew only the Bible, together with the semi-mystical speculation of Valentin

Weigel (1533-1588), which made the Scriptures more myth than record of actual fact. Böhme was sensitive to the scattered nature of visible things, as his horoscope indicates, and he came to believe that a great mystery must be involved. In three great splashlike revelations he penetrated to the inner center of nature, and learned how to see through to the innermost heart of creatures at a glance. Here is a significant manifestation of the *splash* type in its characteristic universality.

Böhme can be said to be one of the great prophets of the modern age, but just exactly what is implied by such a statement? The word "prophet" primarily means one who speaks for another, or an individual who somehow in his words or person represents the purposes, ideals and accomplishments of a community, a nation or a people. This is what is meant when Moses or Mohammed is identified by the word. Böhme's name has been elevated far above those of men whose work was perhaps more important in the rise of modern mysticism or occultism, such as Meister Eckhart, simply because his own life and person conspired with his writings to erect a unique or prophetic figure, and so capture the imagination of men. It is not important that Böhme be the historical cause of any widespread belief in a universal or cosmic consciousness, but only that he give dignity to this concept, and contribute reality to its effectiveness as a way of life. People who sharply illustrate the seven simple types of temperament-set are prophets among men because they dramatize human potentialities in a particularly distinctive way, and because the study and analysis of their lives is a living or continually reconstructive inspiration to others.

Obviously there are more than seven prophets in history, and more than seven prophetic types. Thus the horoscopes of Abdul Baha, Emanuel Swedenborg and Mary Baker G. Eddy are among the example charts of this text. All three were founders or pioneer protagonists of important world-wide religious movements, of which they were prophets. Yet no one of the three is an ideal illustration of a primary type in this mode of identification, such as Böhme here, or Oliver Cromwell in a following chapter. Classification is necessarily arbitrary. It is a tool of the understanding.

All men are composites of a myriad or more factors in character, situation and general potentiality, and yet all of them are equally simple and outstanding in some one respect. The fact that an individual may be a borderline case in the present sevenfold analysis merely means that he partakes of two or more general potentialities. These are made understandable by their special dramatization in the more ideal illustrations. The prophets of these distinctions are therefore archetypes. They are pattern figures which the astrologer uses as an aid in understanding the particular possibilities of a given life. Men are classified by their approach to the simple or archetypal extremes, and the interpretation of their horoscopes is guided by a realization of the extent to which they deviate from the archetypal pattern, or of the degree to which they participate in several various lines of general potentiality. The figures who are employed for illustrative purposes are therefore of prophetic stature in a double sense. They are selected not only because they are prophets in their own right, but also because they are, conveniently, the prophets of these seven specially important astrological distinctions.

A warning is necessary in connection with the use of the three planets discovered in modern times, in the horoscopes of individuals who have lived the whole or any appreciable part of their lives prior to the years these bodies were discovered. This means 1781 for Uranus, 1846 for Neptune and 1930 for Pluto. Astrological theory finds meaning in the planets as they are related to human experience. The discovery of these new bodies coincides with the expansions in human capacity and understanding to which their rulership is properly given. When they are taken into account in older horoscopes, they must be understood to indicate developments significant to these later periods.

Jacob Böhme had nothing in his own consciousness to which any of the three new planets might correspond, in view of the fact that he died in 1624, but the historical influence of any character of importance is centered only incidentally in the personal life of the man himself. The horoscope of an outstanding individual reveals the living or continuing contribution to which his life was an impetus, and for which his name stands. In Böhme's own age the judgment given here of his work would not have been possible, and his achievement could not have had the significance it has acquired in events reaching on down into the present age. As a matter of fact, no character in past history can ever be known in the true terms of his actual environment, but only as later minds reconstruct his reality in their own experience. In the case of Pluto, the discovery is so recent that to put the planet in the charts of prominent people is a meaningless gesture, unless it is to reveal them and their influence in the milieu of a vastly transformed world.

Another example of the *splash* type, as it falls away from the *splash* ideal, is found in the horoscope of Immanuel Kant.

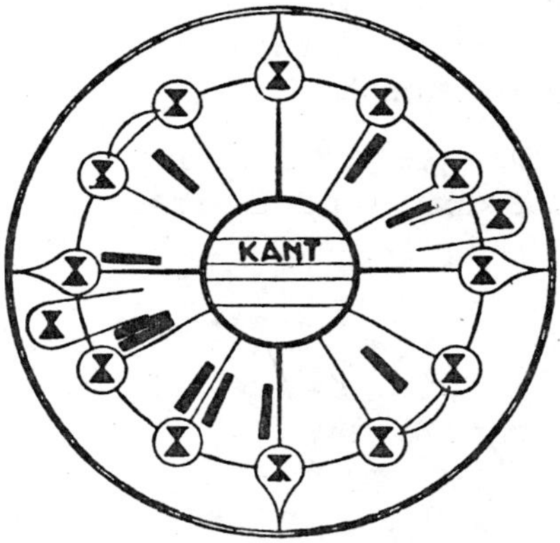

Here the distribution of the planets is not as even or as scattered as in the case of Böhme. There are four empty houses instead of three and two of the four are adjacent. Moreover, there are two houses which contain two planets apiece, instead of the one in Böhme's chart. The distribution through the signs, however, shows that the falling away from the ideal is not as great as might appear to the superficial glance, because the planets range through eight signs instead of seven, as in Böhme's case, and only two of them are in conjunction, in contrast with three in the Böhme horoscope. This one conjunction has a fairly wide orb.

Immanuel Kant presents the *splash* type of universality with an achievement on the scientific rather than the mystical side of speculation. He founded the German idealism which has transformed the entire modern world, indirectly if not literally, and the extent to which he stands a prophet among men is shown by the ease with which philosophy can be divided, on the basis of his work, as "before Kant" in the definite medieval tradition, and "after Kant" in the modern development resulting from the idealistic movement.

A further example of the *splash* type, as it falls away from the *splash* ideal, is found in the horoscope of Richard Wagner.

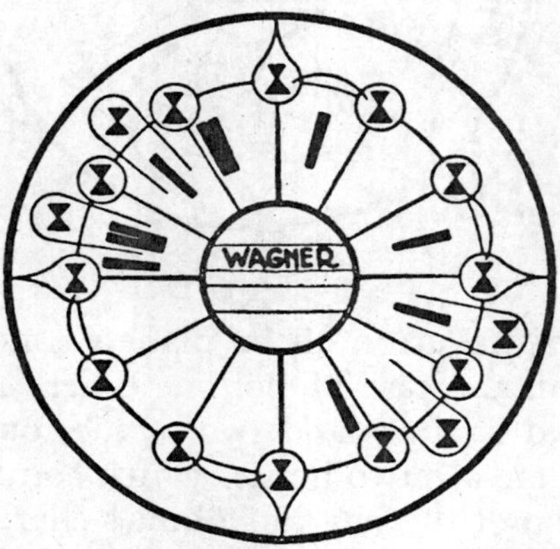

Here the apparent great distance between the planets on the cusps of the first and fifth houses is not a trine, as it appears, but a fairly close sextile. This shows the danger in making too fine a distinction on the basis of a mere glance. Wagner's chart leans away from the *splash* ideal, but it presents only four empty houses and an equal number of empty signs. The three adjacent empty houses raise the question of the classification. There are only two cases of planets in conjunction, with the orb very wide in one.

Richard Wagner, one of the greatest of prophets in music, offers a spectacular illustration of the *splash* temperament. His scattering led him to reach out into stagecraft as well as composition, into an abandon of libretto which paralleled an almost cosmic sense of orchestration. His music-drama was at once a mystical revelation suggestive of Böhme, and a new philosophy of experience as epochal as the work of Kant.

An example of the *splash* type, as it approaches the ideal extreme among contemporary or near-contemporary figures, is found in the horoscope of Theodore Roosevelt.

Here the planets are distributed through eight of the twelve houses, and eight of the twelve signs. Only two houses contain more than one planet. Of the two instances in which more than one planet is found in a sign, Mercury and the sun are in conjunction, but Uranus and Jupiter are widely spaced. No conjunctions are formed over the boundary line between any two signs. The distribution in general is as even as in the chart of Jacob Böhme, and this should indicate that Theodore Roosevelt, like the German mystic, has a special genius for a broad spread out into the affairs of life. As a matter of fact, this is one characteristic for which the American president was noted. His interest in nearly everything, his delight in a personal acquaintance with practically everybody, was the basis of much raillery at the peak of his influence. His gift for scattering was shown in his attack on those he colorfully labeled "malefactors of great wealth", in his strengthening of the navy, in his exceptional service to conservation, in his building of the Panama Canal with some perhaps high-handed international procedures, in a host of other activities; all excellent demonstration of a universal ordering by a *splash* individual at his best.

The focal determinators in any horoscope are illuminated by this classification according to the basic temperament-set, here the *splash* type, and at the same time they confirm and expand the original insight into the nature of the chart, as this is gained by an initial recognition of its place among the seven general possibilities. The focal determinators in the Roosevelt chart are the two cosmic-cross configurations. The reader new to astrology may have to turn to Appendix B for a list and description of these determinators, but he will find them explained by ample illustrations as he follows the astrological delineations through the course of the text.

The T cross in common signs dominates Roosevelt's horoscope, indicating his fundamental interest in people or personal relations. In any T cross the direction of energies lies at the short rather than the long axis of the relationship, or is always distributed in principal part by the planet in square relation with the other two. Neptune is at the short axis in this T cross, intercepted and retrograde. The emphasis of Neptune, the planet of obligation, shows that President Roosevelt acts almost entirely under the compulsion of the general social situation, or is impelled by the special needs of his era and its conflicts. This is confirmed, in double fashion, by the interception and retrogradation of Neptune. Both these factors indicate a more subjective control of a given activity, interception in the realm of circumstances because it is a phenomenon of the houses, and retrogradation in the area of function because it takes place in the signs.

The T cross in fixed signs is completed by Pluto, and consequently it did not operate in the native's own lifetime. The point of stimulus at the short axis, Saturn in Leo, identifies a deep realization which becomes evident to the American people through the 1929 transition. The

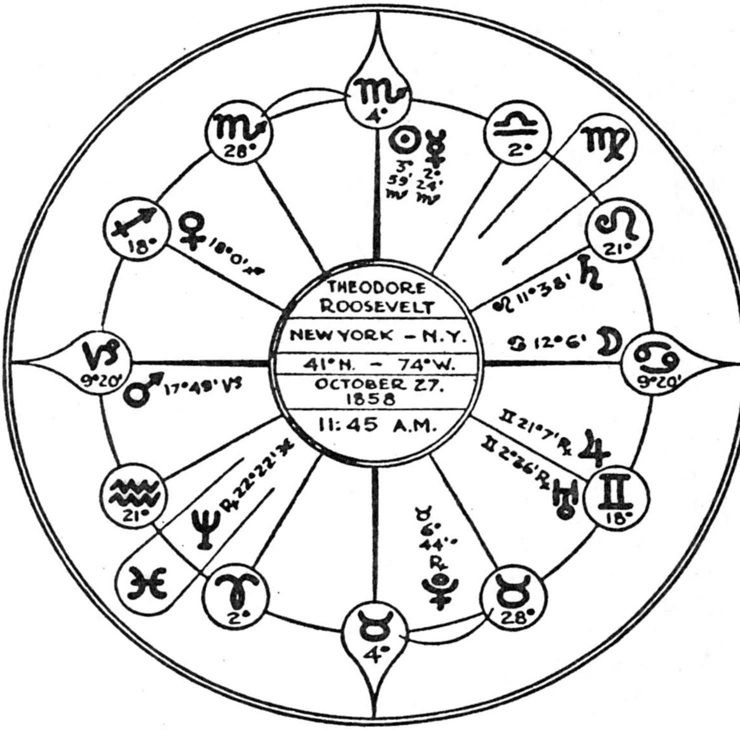

influence of Roosevelt persists in his contribution to ideas and values, under the fixed signs. In other words, he built far more wisely than he himself could ever suspect, consciously. His contribution to American life begins to take on real significance ten years after his death, and this shows that his life should be studied principally in the light of what he was able to do, superlatively, in fitting the United States to meet the challenge to its existence under the order of things to which Pluto corresponds. The imperialism to which he seemed to contribute, in his own day, becomes the foundation for a new international responsibility after 1930, or when the underlying concept of American life changes, and can be revealed by this focal determinator in the life of a real prophet in international politics. Meanwhile, in the other cosmic cross, the position of Neptune as the point of stimulus in the house of possessions is a sharp indication of Roosevelt's universal or Neptunian concern with all possible resources, and this is also and instantly revealed by the *splash* pattern of the chart as a whole.

A second example of the *splash* type among contemporary or near-contemporary figures, and an illustration of deviation from the ideal extreme, is found in the horoscope of Leon Trotsky.

Here the distribution is not as even as in the preceding example. The tenth house, and the sign Taurus, contain three planets, which is a marked falling away from the ideal type. However, the seven other planets are in seven other signs and houses, so that this horoscope definitely classifies in the *splash* pattern. Indeed, only two of the planets in Taurus are in conjunction. Leon Trotsky is another example of a wide spread in interest, with few public inhibitions. In a way already exemplified by the lives of Böhme, Kant, Wagner and Roosevelt, he created for himself a splendid whole world of his own making. Of the original group of Bolsheviks who gathered around Nikolay Lenin to carry out the theories of Karl Marx in the Russian experiment, he alone remained faithful to the original vision of the world revolution as an ultimate scattering in all social relations. Up to the time of his

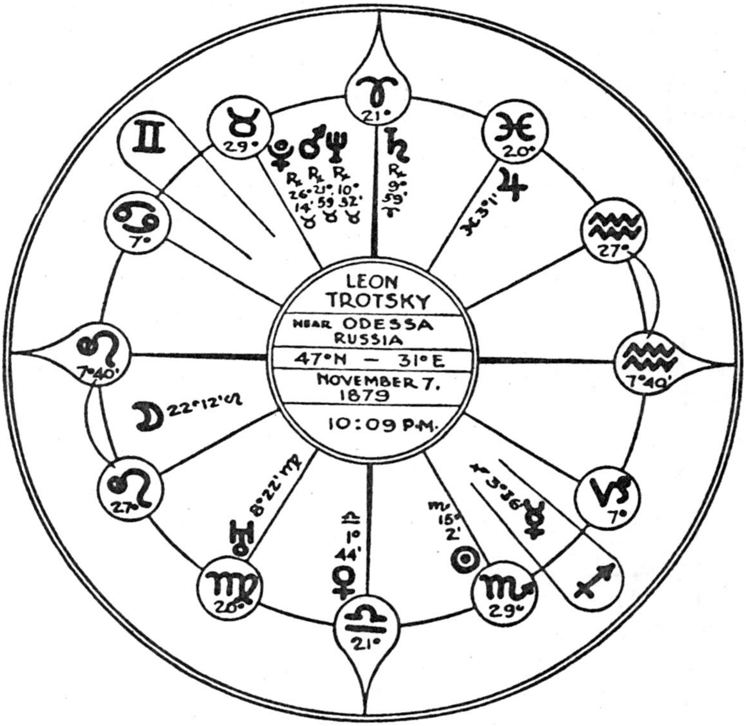

death he sought consistently to bring it to pass, with no thought of the temporizing which characterized the policies of Lenin himself, and of Joseph Stalin. Trotsky's brilliance as a military organizer and leader is an excellent demonstration of the *splash* genius. The difference between his career and that of Lenin or Stalin is revealed by his horoscope in contrast with the charts of the other two, the data for which is given in Appendix C.

An examination of Trotsky's horoscope shows the first focal determinator to be a strong T cross in common signs. This links him with Theodore Roosevelt in his concern over people, and in his belief that the world's problems are solved on a basis of personality. An almost equally strong T cross in fixed signs accounts for his interest in the Marxist philosophy, his distinctly utopian temperament and his willingness to sacrifice his life for an abstract cause. The fact that two cosmic crosses as strong as these are found functioning in one chart indicates the tendency toward general diffusion which the *splash* pattern reveals more quickly. The unusually high emphasis of the scattering is a reflection of the conflict between the two crosses. Moreover, the influence of Pluto, discovered in Trotsky's later life, has a tendency to complete the X form of the common cross. This X cross is often a most unfortunate indication of diffusive and non-co-ordinated efforts, so that Trotsky's achievement might have been impossible in the new era inaugurated by Pluto. What is evil in one respect, however, may be good in another. Though Trotsky lost his chance in his spread of himself, his cause cost him his life and he became a martyr. In death he may be a greater prophet, serving as an ideal of universal values to an extent he never achieved in life. The points of stimulus in his two T crosses are found in Mercury and the moon, and his conceptions and his public impact may be stronger than ever. Certainly the extreme emphasis of a scattering genius may have a greater manifestation in this new way.

A third example of the *splash* type among contemporary or near-contemporary figures, and an illustration of deviation from the ideal extreme, is found in the horoscope of Stephen Foster.

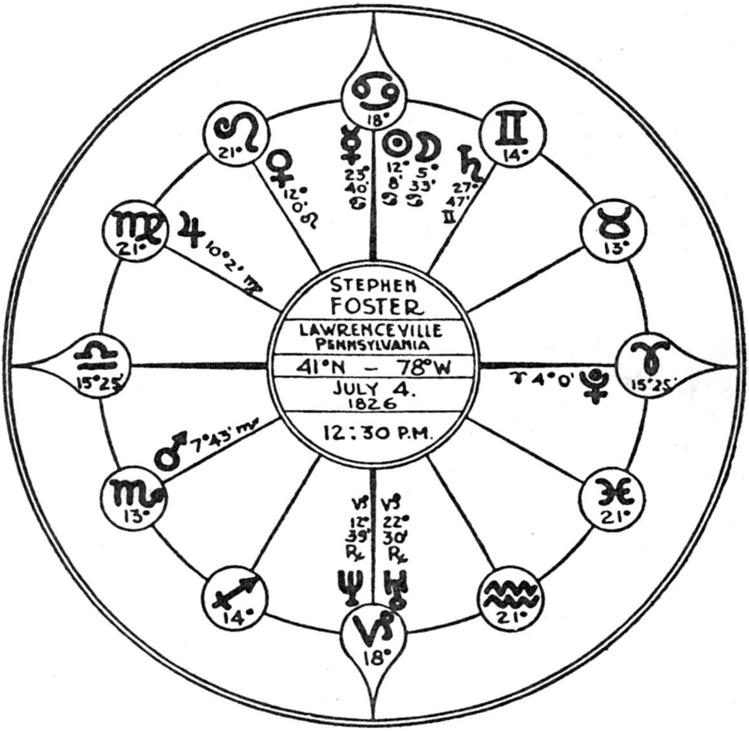

Here the *splash* pattern begins to blend into several other classifications, according to the taste of the individual astrologer, but it is yet essentially an example of the scatter temperament, and in some respects an excellent one. Thus seven of the twelve houses contain planets, and only two of them more than one. In the ninth house, where three planets are placed, only two are in the same sign. However, five of the signs are devoid of planets, and three planets, including the two lights, are found in Cancer, giving Cancer a special emphasis above the others. On top of all this, the planets in Cancer are opposed by two in Capricorn, creating a strong axis on the midheaven line and breaking away from the more simple universality of the ideal *splash* type. Stephen Foster is the true prophet of the American folk melody, far more than Dvořák, because the people themselves have taken his songs and made them their own. His scatter is in his sense of life's unlimited rhythm in this new world, and in the ultimate ineffectiveness of his own personal career in any success-story terms. He lives on, a man of all peoples and all times although the American scene gives him his materials. The universal nature of his appeal is revealed by Pluto, the planet that determines the focus of his chart, and this shows that the real appreciation for his compositions is yet to come.

The focal determination, without Pluto, is found in the clustering of the planets around the midheaven axis. This indicates a person more wrapped up in his achievement than in his personal welfare, superficially a carefree soul, going and coming with his creative impulses and so personally irresponsible or scattered. With Pluto's discovery the life is revealed in its more ordered and universal set, and this is the man immortalized in his songs. The chart now reveals the universal genius, but shows it as it comes closer to the other basic types. There is a *splash* personality here, but the scatter is pinned down to some extent. The pinning, at the meridian axis, is strengthened by a T cross in cardinal signs, completed by Pluto as the point of stimulus. This configuration shows the degree to which Foster prophetically senses the struggles, the needs, the aspirations of human beings, black and white together.

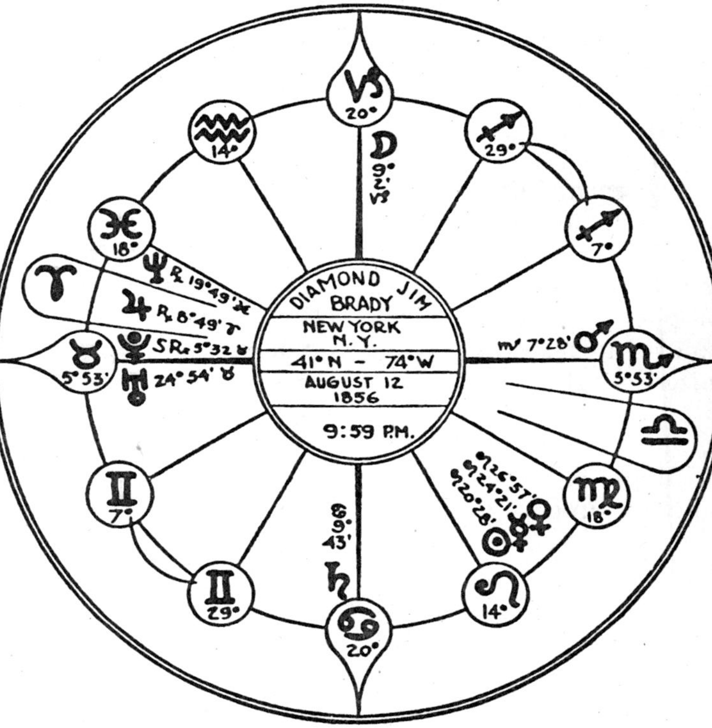

A fourth example of the *splash* type among contemporary or near-contemporary figures, and an illustration of deviation from the ideal extreme, is found in the horoscope of James Buchanan Brady, more familiarly known as Diamond-Jim Brady.

Here the planets are moving away from the *splash* type in quite a different fashion, tending to aggregate in several significant groups rather than to form the central axis found in Stephen Foster's case. Planets are placed in six houses and seven signs, and the only conjunctions are in Leo where the sun, Mercury and Venus, never far apart, are gathered together within seven degrees. Only two of the empty houses are adjacent, and only two of the unoccupied signs. While two houses contain three planets each, only two signs contain more than one planet. This is definitely a borderline case, since other classifications of the chart are possible, but the *splash* identification remains the most revealing. Diamond-Jim Brady is the prophet of American salesmanship at its most glamorous point. Indeed, no character in modern business has epitomized or glorified the lowly drummer as splendidly as Brady. His sales were in terms of very large orders, made to very few customers, so that his spending account had no limit. His sales record was such that he functioned without supervision. In consequence, and with the unlimited funds at his disposal, he became the almost legendary playboy of Broadway. His scattering eclipsed all others of his day, and this more or less prodigal side of his career has obscured his gift of salesmanship, which reveals the *splash* pattern in its happier aspect.

The focal determinators in this horoscope are an exceptionally strong cardinal T cross, and an absence of emphasis in air signs. The cardinal cross places the center of Brady's interest in the issues and crises around him, giving him his love for the excitement of the Gay Nineties. Its point of stimulus is in the expansive Jupiter, but Jupiter's position is in the twelfth house, a place of restriction, where it is intercepted and retrograde like Theodore Roosevelt's Neptune. He does not have Roosevelt's sense of compulsion in his life work, since the Jupiter focus is more spontaneous than Neptune's, but he senses the thrice-subjective nature of his own deeper impulses. They make him uncomfortable, and stir him to action. He cannot bare his own soul to others, even if he desires, but he can find himself in the scattering by which he becomes the soul of Times Square, and thereby leads men to believe it is necessary to be distinguished, even in Gargantuan dissipation under Jupiter. His lack of air emphasis confirms his handicap in true self-expression, and makes him feel it necessary to do more than his part at all times, in order to justify himself in his basic *splash* instincts.

CHAPTER TWO

THE BUNDLE TYPE

NEXT among the simple patterns the planets may form around the zodiac, in contrast with the greatest diffusion or evenness of distribution in the scattered or *splash* type, is the exact reverse, or a concentration of all these bodies in one place. The ideal of an actual tenfold conjunction may never be encountered, but the approach to the possibility is an obvious type of temperament. Although this is the least common of the seven basic differentiations, it is one of the most interesting, and its characteristic is the bunching of interests or the intensive self-gathering which is least responsive to any universal stimulus. The *bundle* pattern is the case where all the planets are within the space of a trine aspect. This often involves a stellium, but the presence of a stellium in a chart does not necessarily indicate a classification under this type. Thus the case of stellium best known to astrologers, that of Louis Pasteur, the data for which may be found in Appendix C, cannot come under the *bundle* pattern because the four planets outside the stellium of six are spread out until the total span comes within the orb of an opposition.

The *bundle* type has a convenient and outstanding illustration in the horoscope of Benito Mussolini.

Here the planets are found in four of the twelve houses, and they also lie within the exact trine formed by the two outermost ones. Thus they occupy the space of four signs although actually placed in five. This is the easiest of all

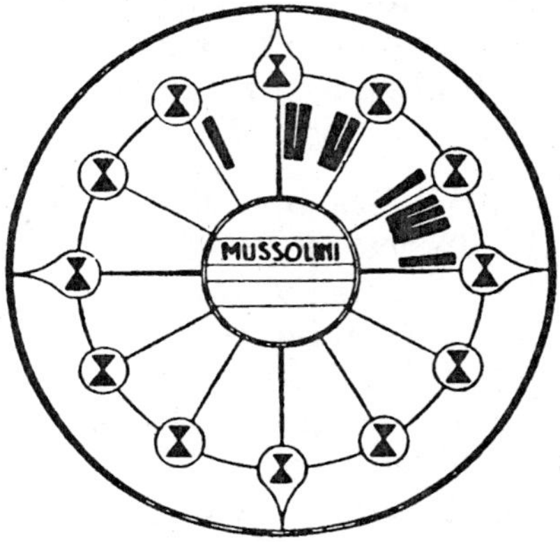

the temperament-sets to recognize or classify. The meaning of the concentration of ten planets in one single third of the zodiac is that the course of a native's life is held to certain narrow bounds of opportunism. He is almost completely inhibited, in contrast with the outstanding lack of inhibition in the *splash* pattern.

Benito Mussolini is the prophet of sheer opportunism for Western civilization. He provides a typical figure, at its somewhat ruthless extreme, to illustrate this one of the seven simple types of human genius. It is his not altogether enviable distinction, on the very threshold of the contemporary scene, to be the archetype of dictators in the popular mind. His regime introduced Fascism to the world. He directly encouraged the rise of Adolf Hitler in Germany, and Francisco Franco in Spain. This does not mean, however, that these men possess horoscopes similar to his. Their patterns of achievement have a different fundamental direction, as can be observed by the interested students through a detailed examination of their charts, the data for which is given in Appendix C. By the same token, the classification of a native under the *bundle* type does not mean he must express his genius for opportunism in Mussolini's fashion, as will be demonstrated in detail.

Mussolini like Böhme, through the long perspective of centuries, is the archetype for a certain type of human personality. Characteristic of the *bundle* type is an outstanding capacity for making much of little, or for building small beginnings into great and often unanticipated final results. Mussolini's life is valuable to the astrologer, not for the part he plays in Italian history, but for his dramatization of the way in which a total world may be molded by some highly centralized force of self-concentration. This phenomenon is the exact contrary to the gift for universal orientation, encountered in the *splash* pattern. Böhme brings the universe to center, but Mussolini takes a little central point in self and makes a vital impact upon the entire world around him.

All over-simplification must be avoided in these comparisons. The extreme contrast made between Böhme and Mussolini is on the basis of an arbitrary distinction, a convenience of classification. The difference exists in life, and is actual, but the importance of this difference is its usefulness to the human mind, as a means for orientation in the analysis. Böhme and Mussolini might also be found exactly alike under some other mode of classification, where other types of difference are brought forward.

Another example of the *bundle* type, as it falls away from the *bundle* ideal, is found in the horoscope of Eduard Beneš.

Here the planets have returned to points within the same confining trine of Mussolini's chart, in an almost

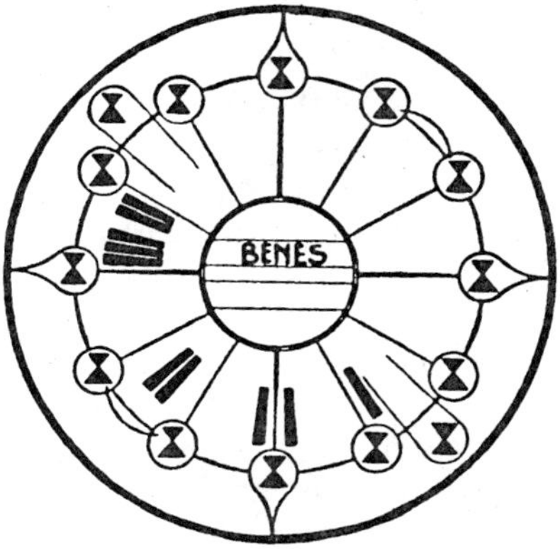

exact duplication of the Italian's general pattern, despite the fact that Beneš was born a year later. The piano-key form of wheel shows a distribution not at all as centralized in the houses, although the sign situation is practically identical. While Mussolini has ten planets confined to four houses, Beneš has them placed through a span of six, with one empty. The charts in their detail are strikingly different, but in the sevenfold pattern-groups they are quite alike, a fact which dramatizes the effective guidance to horoscope interpretation afforded by the typing.

Eduard Beneš was the leader of Czechoslovakia through the tragic events in that young nation's history, when the Fascism fathered initially by Mussolini was rising to its full world-sweep. Before that, he had labored significantly with President Masaryk in the establishment and strengthening of the Central European democracy. The differences, as well as the likenesses, of Beneš and Mussolini are an illustration of the nature of this temperament of which the Italian is a prophet. Fundamentally the Czech sought to solve his problems with the same disregard for ultimate considerations which has characterized the other; both have been opportunistic. But despite this similarity in the temperament of the two men, one contributed to democracy as consistently as the other built an entrenched authoritarianism.

A further example of the *bundle* type, as it falls away from the *bundle* ideal, is found in the horoscope of Pierre Laval.

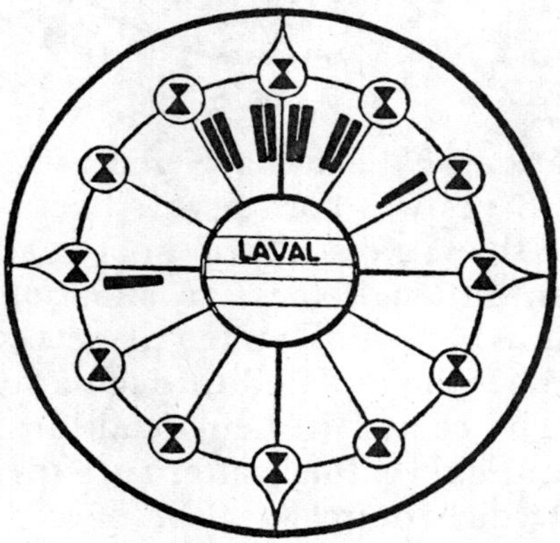

Here the planets have all moved close to one side of the confining trine, giving a stellium which neither of the other two figures possesses, although Laval's birthday is near Mussolini's, in the same year. Moreover, one planet has passed outside the confining trine by a little over a sign, enough so that the chart might be classified differently by some astrologers. Nonetheless Pierre Laval can best be understood as a *bundle* type because the concentration of planets is unusually marked in the case of all but one, and this one is definitely linked to the aggregation by the trine dominating so many horoscopes of the early 1880's.

Pierre Laval as a personality is a relatively minor figure, only of importance in connection with the rise of the Fascist spirit in Europe, and with his attempt to contribute to its acceptance in France. His method was the same although his policy was the reverse of that adopted by Benes. He did not have a capacity to win public support, characteristic of the other, and in consequence he was not able to play as much the prophet's rôle as the Czechoslovakian leader. His lesser measure of success has nothing to do with the fact that he is a borderline case in the classification, but is the result of the use he makes of the potentialities revealed by his chart as a whole.

An example of the *bundle* type as it approaches the ideal extreme, among contemporary or near-contemporary figures, is found in the horoscope of William James.

Here the planets are concentrated in four houses and four signs, a much tighter aggregation than in Mussolini's case. The outermost planets can almost be considered in a square; indeed, are closer to that aspect than to the trine which defines the *bundle* pattern. If Pluto is eliminated the clustering is even more remarkable, showing the situation which prevails in the lifetime of James. The position of the moon is unknown, since no time of birth is available, but its range of possible place is indicated and it will be noted that it cannot leave the stellium in Capricorn. The form of horoscope is the solar chart, often employed when no hour of birth is available.

William James is pre-eminently the prophet of the practical American way of life, and by many is thought to be the greatest thinker America has produced. The philosophy he developed with Charles Saunders Peirce, continued by John Dewey and his followers, is known as pragmatism, from the Greek word for business. James demanded that all things be considered in terms of their cash value, or the immediate pertinency which is characteristic of the *bundle* point of view. The self-intentness of this type has already been illustrated in terms of political action, and it is also revealed in the hypochondria which James exhibited through most of his life.

An outstanding focal determinator of the horoscope is the stellium in Capricorn. It indicates the native's great gift for solving problems, or for seeing the potentials of life in the terms of the immediate situation and its significance. Another focal determinator of equal importance is the fact that Saturn is a singleton by disposition. As a result the concentration of the philosopher's consciousness in the Capricorn "fix-it" genius is much stronger than is the case with Louis Pasteur, whose stellium is also in Capricorn. The emphasis of Saturn gives James the depth of understanding which enables him to visualize a pluralistic world, a reality squared to the American scene with its open frontiers or unending opportunities ever ahead.

A second example of the *bundle* type among contemporary or near-contemporary figures, and an illustration of deviation from the ideal extreme, is found in the horoscope of Queen Elizabeth of Rumania, the author known best under her pen name of Carmen Sylva.

Here the concentration of planets in four signs parallels the charts of Mussolini and James. Although almost a full two years separate the births of the queen and the American philosopher, her horoscope is like his in the fact of its Capricorn stellium, and the position of its Saturn as a singleton in disposition. But thereupon likeness ends. Only four planets make up her stellium, instead of six,

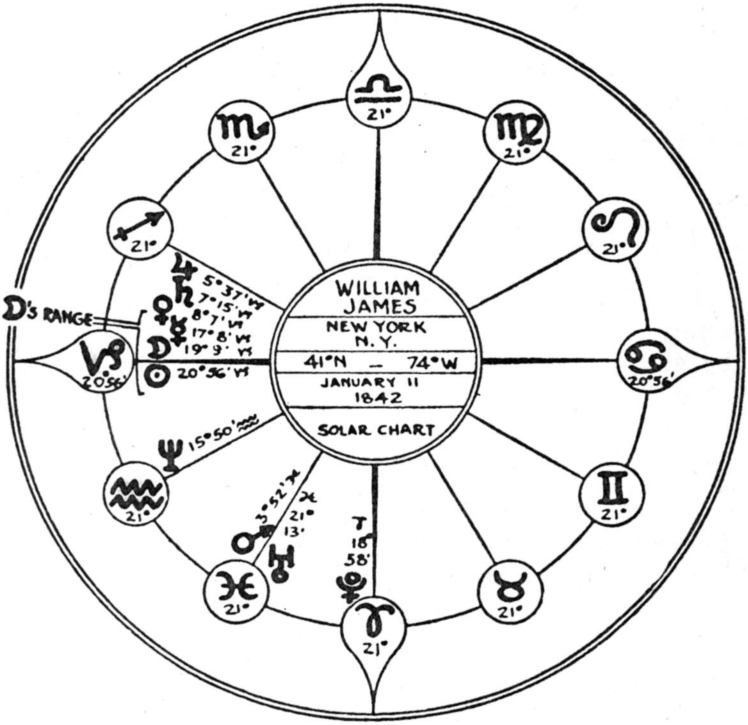

and it is only a stellium exceptionally, through the strength of its Saturn, since the other three planets are the sun and its two consistently close companions. There are additional focal determinators in an eastern and also a southern hemisphere-emphasis, indicating respectively that she is able to take conscious control of her destiny, and that her life is fundamentally lived in an objective or frank and open fashion. The latter hemisphere-emphasis is not negated by the presence of the rising planet a few degrees below the horizon, since allowance must be made, in most horoscopes of celebrities, for a time of birth only known approximately.

Elizabeth of Neuwied, Carmen Sylva's real name, was the daughter of a German princeling. By marriage she was first crown princess and then queen of the country for whom she was to do much by becoming its living prophet. She collected its folklore, encouraged its arts and crafts, and gained wide recognition for its culture. Her *bundle* pattern, as narrow as that of James in its general planetary concentration, is well exemplified in the gradual process by which she worked out from the intensified center of her self-concern into a social and literary career, ultimately touching the whole world on a solid if somewhat modest scale.

The third example of the *bundle* type among contemporary or near-contemporary figures, and an illustration of deviation from the ideal extreme, is found in the horoscope of America's colorful self-styled "king of the hobos", Jeff Davis.

Here is a case where the planets spread out beyond the basic trine by twenty degrees, in contrast with the seventeen degrees less than an exact trine found in the charts of both William James and Carmen Sylva. The tendency of the *bundle* type to shade into other classifications is shown at this point. However, the even distribution of the planets through a third-part of the wheel, defined loosely by the mundane trine of Taurus-Virgo, makes the *bundle* classification a first choice. Not a great deal is known about the life of this king of the tramps, but it is not necessary to have many facts in detail. He is simply the prophet of

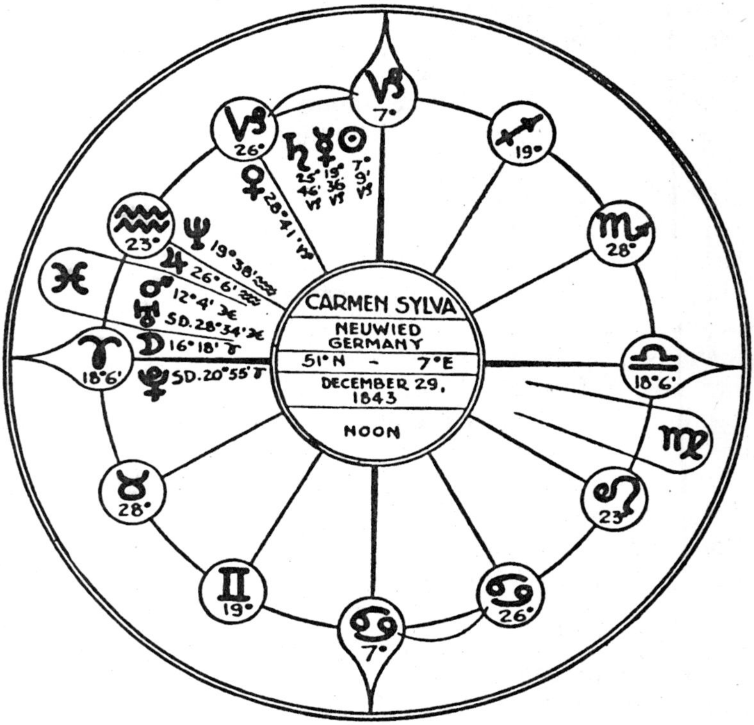

a certain happy-go-lucky temperament which has an interesting place in American life. The hobo above all else is self-intent. He carries his world about in a very special psychological bundle, where he controls it fairly well to his liking.

The outstanding focal determinators in the chart may be taken as the singleton moon above the earth, and as the tendency of the planets to form pairs. Both the moon and Neptune are in Taurus and the twelfth house, but planets less than five degrees above the cusp of a house may be taken as situated in that house, and this native definitely shows the influence of a rising Neptune in his tramp temperament. The moon is only technically a singleton since it rests in the rising sign, but it is nonetheless a focal indication, here strengthened because it is elevated and in the sign of its exaltation. It explains the flair for gaining public attention which has marked this hobo king. More important in his horoscope is the tendency of the planets to form pairs, or the preponderance of conjunctions in the particular effectiveness which follows their spacing well apart from each other. This pairing always indicates a gift for doing even little things significantly, and here the tendency is quite marked.

The fourth example of the *bundle* type among contemporary or near-contemporary figures, and an illustration of deviation from the ideal extreme, is found in the horoscope of William McKinley.

Here the planets again lie outside the confining trine, even beyond the signs naturally in trine relation. The narrow concentration of all but Mars and Pluto in the space of a square, together with the fact that Pluto was discovered long after President McKinley's death, makes the *bundle* type a best choice, and gives a valuable illustration of the technique in borderline cases. The life of William McKinley conforms to the *bundle* classification, but he did not display the genius of a Mussolini. He was a prophet of the conformist, and a party man in every respect. What was particularly true of this president, in his manifestation of the *bundle* temperament, was his practi-

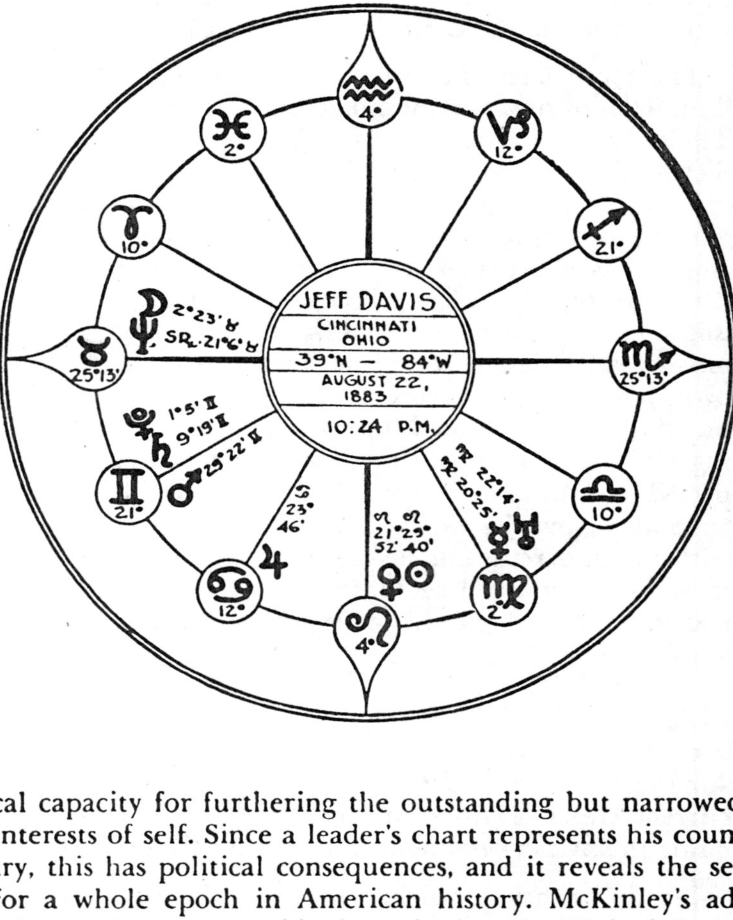

cal capacity for furthering the outstanding but narrowed interests of self. Since a leader's chart represents his country, this has political consequences, and it reveals the set for a whole epoch in American history. McKinley's administration was notable for ushering the United States into a period of self-conscious imperialism. The Spanish-American War was the particular demarking event, but the development was shown in the general business expansion. The appeal to this individualistic or imperialistic and self-seeking impulse was dramatized by McKinley's successful use of the campaign slogan, "a full dinner pail".

The focal determinators in the horoscope are the stellium in Aquarius, and the singleton Pluto above the earth. The stellium is not as strong as in the case of James, and there is no singleton in disposition to give it added strength, but it does indicate McKinley's complacent and somewhat utopian temperament. The singleton Pluto emphasizes the degree to which his epoch lives on in American history, in a surviving and broadening imperialism. Pluto is close to the horizon, which minimizes its force as a singleton. Its continuing emphasis is indicated by its position in the seventh house or place of opportunity, but this holds whether Pluto is a singleton or not. Nothing of his real rôle as a messiah of exploitation was suspected by McKinley in his own lifetime. Then his planets were all below the earth, and his conscious struggle was with the undercurrents he found around him. His career in this respect was like Martin Luther's, who never suspected he was the prophet of an entirely new ecclesiastical development. The data for Luther's horoscope is given in Appendix C, and it may be used in comparison with McKinley's chart, which though not as ideal a *bundle* is yet stronger because the stellium in Aquarius gives the American president a greater practical sense of ordinary current trends. This characteristic would be a primary guide in any personal delineation of McKinley's chart.

Martin Luther illuminates the life of William McKinley because the response to unsuspected trends, at a turning point in the culture, is more obvious in an ecclesiastical context. These individuals and their horoscopes are differ-

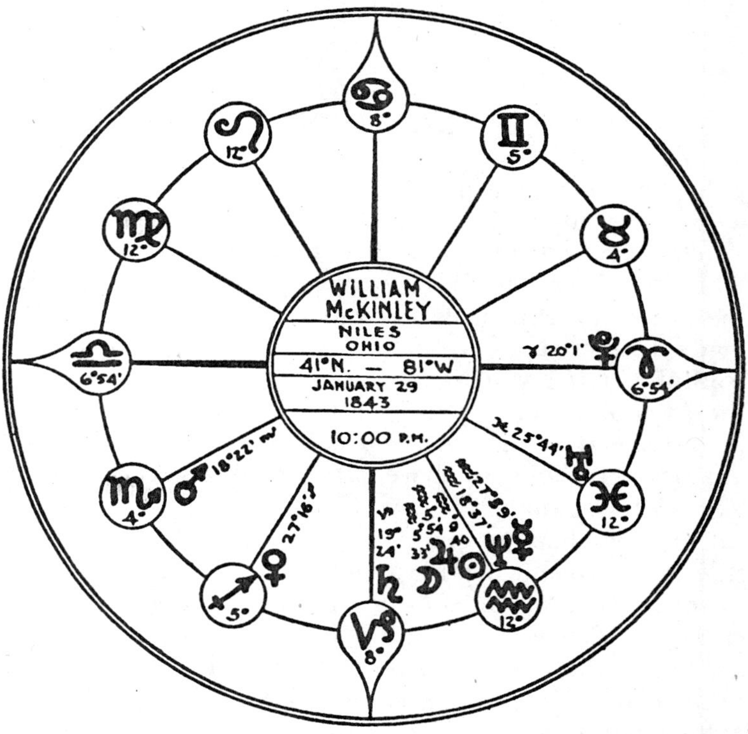

ent at nearly every point of detailed analysis, but Luther's unwitting precipitation of the Reformation in Europe is a clue to the equally important catalysis provided by McKinley's administration for America. While Luther himself was the voice of the new social focus, however, McKinley was rather the sounding board against which the new American spirit significantly found its voice in the person of William Jennings Bryan.

Chapter Three

THE LOCOMOTIVE TYPE

If the concentration of the ten planets of a horoscope within the span of a confining trine is significant, the exactly reversed state of affairs should be significant also. This would be the case where all planets are placed in the other two-thirds of the zodiac, or where the chart is made distinctive by an "empty trine", in contrast with the confining trine which provides the defining measure of the *bundle* pattern. The situation here sets up what may be described as an eccentric balance. There is a rough analogy to the counterweight placed on each driving wheel of a locomotive. It was discovered in early days of railroading that the engine's driving rod, bearing at one side of the wheel when it applied the power from the steam cylinder, had a tendency to defeat the smooth flow of energy by developing a side-thrust, or by contributing to a weaving motion from side to side. This was a strain on both locomotive and rails. It was necessary to place an extra amount of metal on the opposite side of the wheel to preserve a balance.

The *locomotive* type of horoscope reveals a balance of this sort in the life. A third part of things, in a symbolical sense, consisting of a free span in experience, is set against a two-thirds part, embracing a related but limited span in experience. The power lies in the disproportion of these two parts. The basis of the dynamic is found in the native's resulting strong sense of a lack or a need, of a problem to be solved, a task to be achieved in the social and intellectual world around him. The temperament reveals a self-driving individuality, an executive eccentricity that is not queerness or unbalance but rather is power. It exhibits a dynamic and exceptionally practical capacity which is neither the broad universality of the *splash* pattern, nor the special obsession with some particularly narrowed aspect of experience characteristic of the *bundle* people.

This *locomotive* classification is the first under which the self is found to be moved more by external factors in the environment than by aspects of its own character. The point of application for the powers of the self is shown very definitely in this class of charts by the "leading planet", or the one of the two in the empty trine which forms its aspect clockwise in the zodiac, irrespective of any distinction as "applying" or "separating". Identification by this pattern at once brings some one planet forward as vital in the analysis.

The *locomotive* type has a convenient and outstanding example in the horoscope of Isaac Newton.

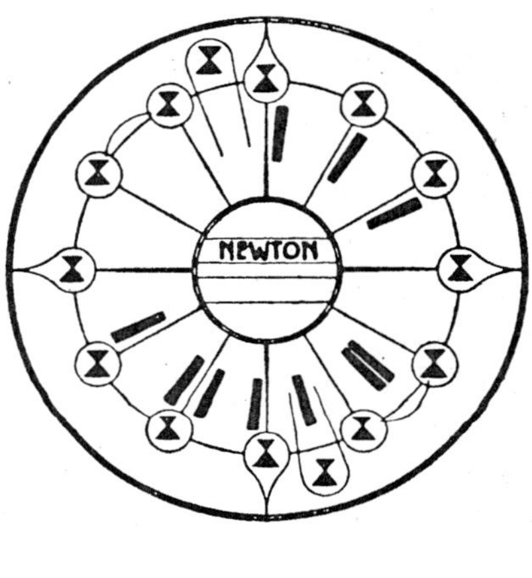

Here the planets are distributed through eight out of the twelve signs and in eight out of the twelve houses, with only one house and one sign empty in the occupied two-thirds segment of the chart. The leading planet is in the first house, and this shows that the point of application of Newton's powers is to the very focus of life itself. It means that his career is essentially personal, or the individualistic achievement characteristic of the late Middle Ages. Also, and more importantly, it indicates his capacity for highly original work. The most vital consequences of his contributions to knowledge, of course, have their full impact in a later generation, as study of the detailed horoscope with the places of the new planets will reveal, but here the chart is an excellent clue to the basic driving force of modern science as a whole, since it is the impetus and not a static contribution which has survived.

Isaac Newton above everything else is the great prophet or embodiment of the scientific spirit. He provides the all-necessary and final intellectual ordering for the achievements of the seventeenth-century speculation, and its world-view based on natural law. What was started by Copernicus and Galileo, and brought to a point where it was ready for Newton's order through the work of Brahe and Kepler, has its completion not only in terms of astronomy but throughout physical science in a new and broad enlightenment. There is driving power not only in Newton's own efforts, but in the momentum to which he gives a special impetus. While the Newtonian contribution in its literal aspect is of lessening moment in today's research, and while Newtonian physics has long since given way to later and more profound intuitions, the prophetic figure yet remains as vital as ever. It is this which illuminates the real genius of the *locomotive* pattern.

Another example of the *locomotive* type, as it falls away from the *locomotive* ideal, is found in the horoscope of George Washington.

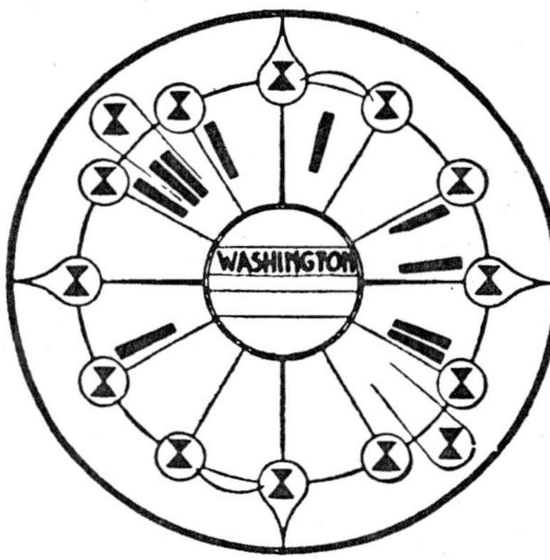

Here the planets are distributed through six houses and eight signs, but with no empty houses or signs adjacent to each other in the occupied two-thirds segment. The leading planet is in the sixth house, and the driving force of this life is directed to the adjustments involved in breaking away from European dominance, and in establishing a new nation. The sweep of the empty trine is across the nadir, so that Washington's influence as a genuine prophet is a subjective matter, an inspiration to inner ideals and spiritual realizations. This emphasis of the lower or northern hemisphere establishes him as the "father of his country".

America's first president is prophetic in the degree to which he captured the imagination of later generations, and enabled them to enshrine their hopes and ideals in his personality; and with the help of Mason Weems to make him an almost mythical figure of absolute perfection. He had his outstanding faults, but these have been overshadowed by the locomotive power of his achievement. Although his planets are not as ideally spaced as Newton's, he yet no less has been a towering major figure in modern history, and this again is testimony to the genius of the pattern.

A further example of the *locomotive* type, as it falls away from the *locomotive* ideal, is found in the horoscope of Mary Baker G. Eddy.

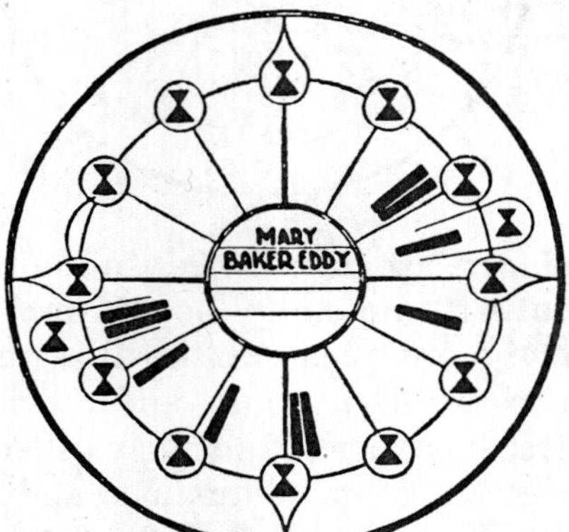

Here the planets are distributed through seven houses and seven signs, actually with about as even a distribution as prevails in the two preceding examples. However, the chart establishes a house arrangement which tends to divide Mrs. Eddy's planets into two sharply distinguished groups, and the defining empty trine is very wide. The classification is justified by the unmistakable *locomotive* patterning, marked by the evenness of the distribution in the two-thirds segment when this is taken in terms of degrees in the signs. The leading planet in Mrs. Eddy's case is one of the newly discovered bodies active in her lifetime, and it is an excellent indicator of her essentially modern contribution to American religious philosophy. Its position in the ascendant, as in Newton's horoscope, shows the personal nature of her achievement.

Mrs. Eddy is the prophet of a modern realistic subjectivism, or of a practical rather than theoretical transcendence. She provided something the common man could realize in his everyday experience, and made this a living tradition with a locomotive power of persistence. Christian Science went into the courts, and compelled a respect for the occult point of view in a way the least of believers might appreciate. Her prophetic stature is demonstrated by the vitality of her own movement, and also by the many others which have sprung from it. If Newton is the prophet of the modern scientific spirit, and Washington the voice of modern democracy, Mrs. Eddy is high priestess for man's recovery of his creative existence, that is, his power to give the world a set according to his own liking.

An example of the *locomotive* type as it approaches the ideal extreme, among contemporary and near-contemporary figures, is found in the horoscope of Henry Ford.

Here the empty trine is less than the span of an exact aspect, but well within a proper orb. The planets are fairly well spaced through the occupied two-thirds of the chart, in eight houses and seven signs. No empty houses or signs are adjacent to each other outside the empty trine, which gives an approach to the ideal spread in the self's organization. The moon is the leading planet, indicating that the native's point of application for his powers is a matter of public interest or broad social service, and also that people generally will co-operate with his efforts. The driving force of his life rises up and across the ascendant, since his empty trine has the same position found in the horoscopes of Newton and Mrs. Eddy. Henry Ford is rather universally recognized as a prophet of major proportions in modern industrial development, through his perfection of the assembly line and mass-production methods. He dramatized the spirit of his leading moon in his expressed ideal to "put America on wheels", or make it possible for even the lowliest worker to have an automobile. He has demonstrated the efficiency of the *locomotive* type in the increasing self-sufficiency of his manufacturing organization, as well as in his instrumenting of a social idealism through his voluntary giving of high wages and a willingness at one time to operate on the basis of a single dollar's earning on each car. His prophetic gift for embodying important ideas in himself, and in his enterprises, is illustrated by his Dearborn Village, with its museum and his preservation there of the Thomas A. Edison memorabilia, and by his entire self-conscious realization of his stewardship in the fortune he has earned.

The focal determination in Ford's chart is unusually marked by its four outstanding features. Two of these must be analyzed together. The *locomotive* typing advances the grand trine in air signs to first importance, bringing it into active function even though the planets barely approximate the extremes of orb allowed. This configuration has given Ford his interest in public opinion, and his conviction that he must make his achievements justify themselves at every point. It also indicates his tendency toward widely separated interests. The T cross in fixed signs is much stronger, and would be of much

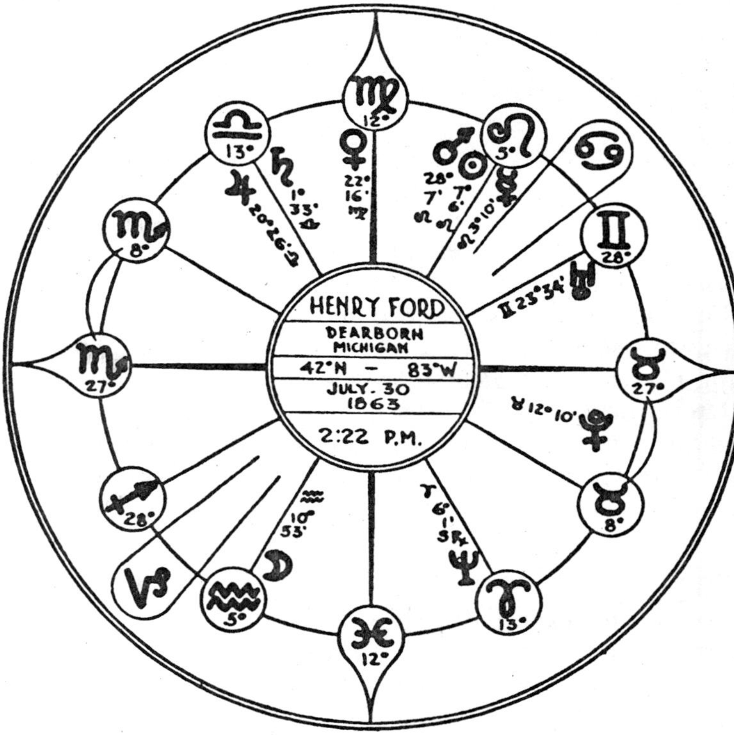

greater importance, except that it is established and given its focus by Pluto. As far as his special activity with ideas and values is concerned, the meaning of a fixed-sign emphasis, this administrative capacity, provided by a cosmic cross, has only been sharpened since the discovery of Pluto in 1930. The grand trine in air by contrast prevails through the whole of his life, marking him as the dreamer. His most important prophetic rôle, however, begins in his sixties. It is established not only through his own life, but much more importantly in the Ford corporation and the general industrial development. Pluto is placed significantly in the house of labor and labor-relations, in the sign of sensitiveness to values or end-results *per se*.

The sun is singleton by disposition, and this gives Ford the high individualism or inherent dignity by which he has been able to maintain his own position, or deep self-orientation, even when circumstances become outwardly ridiculous, as in the case of the famous peace ship in 1915. The sun's emphasis here provides a creative self-sufficiency, a dramatic self-integrity, which greatly enhances the driving power of the *locomotive* type. A fourth point in focal determination is the absence of planetary emphasis in water signs, which suggests Ford's great sense of need for a universal consciousness, or a unifying principle in experience. It is an important factor because the position of the empty trine athwart the water ascendant has encouraged his very practical if substitute universality.

A second example of the *locomotive* type among contemporary or near-contemporary figures, and an illustration of deviation from the ideal extreme, is found in the horoscope of Cecil Rhodes.

Here the empty trine is wide, by slightly more than a degree over the orb usually allowed, and the chart lacks the grand trine which often characterizes the pattern. The distribution of planets is far short of the even-spacing ideal, with the positions concentrated in five houses and six signs. Although none of the three empty houses of the occupied two-thirds section are adjacent, two of the three empty signs are ranged together at the ascendant. This situation illustrates an extreme of classification under the

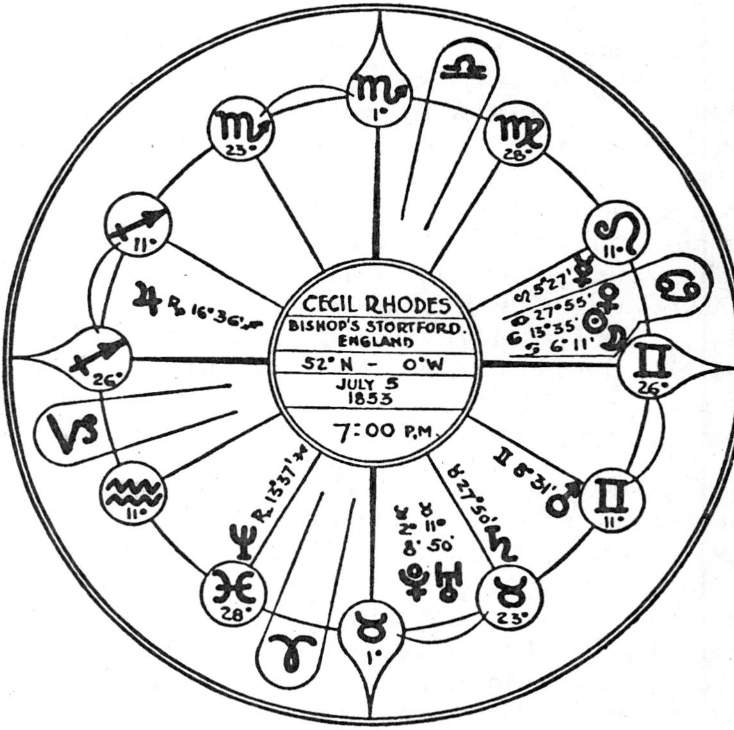

locomotive type, but the identification is justified as the best for the native because Jupiter has a special very high emphasis, and this strengthens it as a possible leading planet. Thus, while the moon disposes of all the direct planets and endows Rhodes with both his capacity and instinct for empire-building, Jupiter disposes of the retrograde group, Neptune and itself, and, by its subjective or twelfth-house position in the rising sign, equips the native with his uncanny skill in uncovering opportunities for exploitation and expansion.

The empty trine, flung across the midheaven, explains the spectacular career in a very simple fashion. Cecil Rhodes is an outstanding "advance man" of civilization in the present age, a prophet of stark imperialism. His influence has been sharpened in the American consciousness by the Rhodes Scholarships, which have selected the cream of all-around American college material over a long period, taking these students to England and there introducing them to the British ideal as this at its best is exemplified by Rhodes himself. His development of South Africa as a field for white-man expansion, excellently illustrating the *locomotive* temperament, was a constructive and far-seeing achievement.

Focal determination is provided by the T cross in common signs, especially significant because Neptune as its point of application indicates Rhodes' close tie with the world trends of his age. There is an emphasis of water and earth signs, which have a natural relationship, over the similarly allied fire and air signs, by seven planets to three. This throws the focus of his life in the direction of universal and social considerations, as against personal self-seeking or abstract theorizing. The common T cross shows his interest in people and their concerns. The general placing of the planets near the horizon and below the earth is a clue to his basic concern over foundations and ultimate ends.

A third example of the *locomotive* type among contemporary or near-contemporary figures, and an illustration of deviation from the ideal extreme, is found in the horoscope of Upton Sinclair.

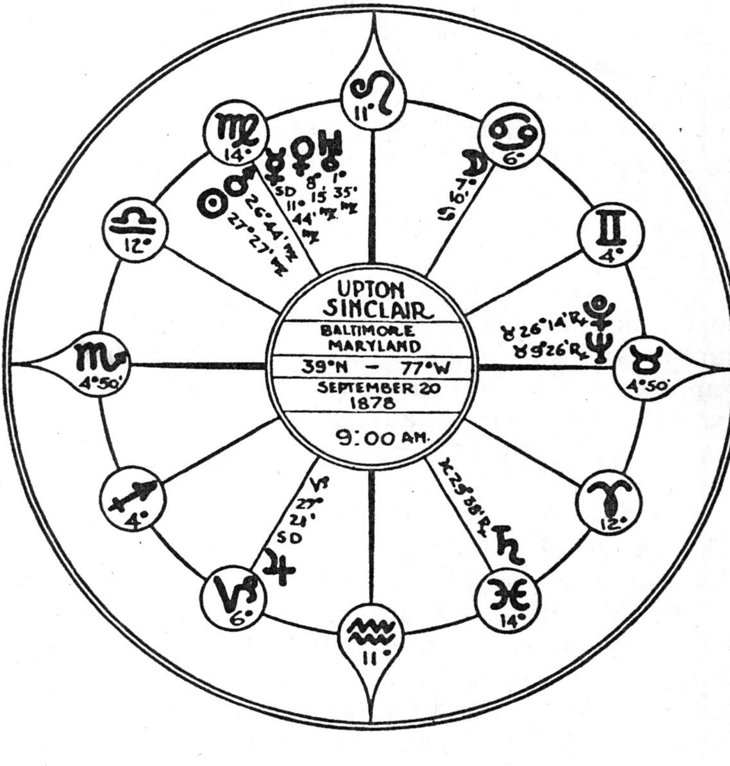

Here the empty trine is exact within six minutes, and Pluto completes the grand trine by aspects almost equally exact to both other planets. The planetary spacing is not at all even, but classification here is suggested by the strength of the defining empty trine. The planets are found in six houses, but with three empty ones in the occupied section, and in only five of the nine signs that constitute the two-thirds segment. The fact that these empty houses and signs are scattered is a justification of *locomotive* classification, as is also the fact that Jupiter, the leading planet, has special importance through its stationary position in turning from retrograde to direct motion. The empty trine throws its dynamic force across the ascendant, as has happened in three other examples of this type, indicating a personal form of pioneering and confirming Jupiter's contribution of expansiveness. Upton Sinclair is a prophet of the crusading temperament, and he has given it expression in literature and in the arts of propaganda. His great achievement was in precipitating the reform of conditions in the Chicago stockyards through the influence of his book *The Jungle*. His busy life, with its unremitting attacks on social evils everywhere, is a striking example of the persistent driving power to be found in the *locomotive* type.

The focal determination is very sharp in this chart. The first detail of importance is a stellium in Virgo. The fact that this is a stellium by sign only is a clue to the essentially functional nature of the native's life, or to an absence of self-seeking which has confirmation in the lack of house emphasis at the first and fourth angles; a further indication of the greater general importance of the sign factors. The heavy preponderance of planets in earth signs, eight of the ten, together with the presence of the other two in the allied water triplicity, is a testimony through the signs to a native's entire freedom from any inner drive by egoistic impulse, always indicated primarily by fire and secondarily by air signs. The Virgo stellium, which gives a pointing to the exceptional ordering instinct here, indicates that he responds principally to the needs for readjustment in everything he contemplates. In other words, what might be Virgo's fussiness on a lesser level becomes, with the *locomotive* emphasis, a cosmic instinct for reform.

Upton Sinclair as a prophet is the very embodiment of propaganda. Unlike Harriet Beecher Stowe, who wrote *Uncle Tom's Cabin* out of her first-hand observation of an immediate and localized wrong, this native must almost of necessity professionalize the exposure of ill and error in every possible direction. His keen capacity for this rôle is strengthened by the rare focal determinator known as a fanhandle, in which some one planet opposes a stellium and gives it a special outlet. Here the planet is Saturn, placed in the house of self-expression. Because Saturn is retrograde, the native works indirectly, or through his writings. He is not as successful as other propagandists in direct exhortation to his fellows, and this confirms what is indicated when there is no planetary emphasis in fire and air signs; that is, a deficient sense of self-competency, leading men to find some substitute self-expression. The moon is the point of stimulus in a T cross which has its base in common signs but which, by this focal planet, is directed into cardinal activity. In such a case the focal planet rather than the quadrature is emphasized, and the consequent importance of the moon accounts for Sinclair's success in awakening public interests. Its place in the ninth house enables him to do this with ideas.

A fourth example of the *locomotive* type among contemporary or near-contemporary figures, and an illustration of deviation from the ideal extreme, is found in the horoscope of George Gershwin.

Here the empty trine is close, whether taken with Neptune in connection with events prior to 1930, or with Pluto subsequently, but one or the other of these is the leading planet, and each must be taken in connection with the proper events of Gershwin's life. At least one secret of his outstanding achievement is this double reference, which enabled him to link the old and the new in his music. The spacing of his planets is relatively even, through seven houses and seven signs, with neither the two empty houses nor the two empty signs of the occupied section adjacent to each other. The placing of the empty trine, as in the Washington chart, shows the degree to which his work dealt with foundations. George Gershwin is the real prophet of an important new development in American music. His life reveals the *locomotive* driving power expressed in musical composition, and the odd Neptune and Pluto leading-planet arrangement indicates his capacity to create an apt beauty or distinction under varying compulsion or on special order, illustrated notably by his "Rhapsody in Blue." The linking of these planets in the empty trine with the moon reveals his flair for catching the popular mood in his melodies. His own life story, in terms of a willingness to undertake hard work, is a real illustration of the *locomotive* temperament.

The focal determinators in this horoscope are the common-sign T cross, with the planet Mercury at its point of stimulus, revealing his warm human interests, and the strong grand trine in air, which indicates his fundamental concern over the general implication of things, greatly strengthening the Mercury focus. The driving power of this life is less prophetic in an everyday sense than is the case with Henry Ford, whose Pluto in the sixth house has enabled him to pour the mold of the new age for labor as much as any man in history. Gershwin has the same grand trine in air as Ford, but not the same general focus of interest and energy. Gershwin's *locomotive* dy-

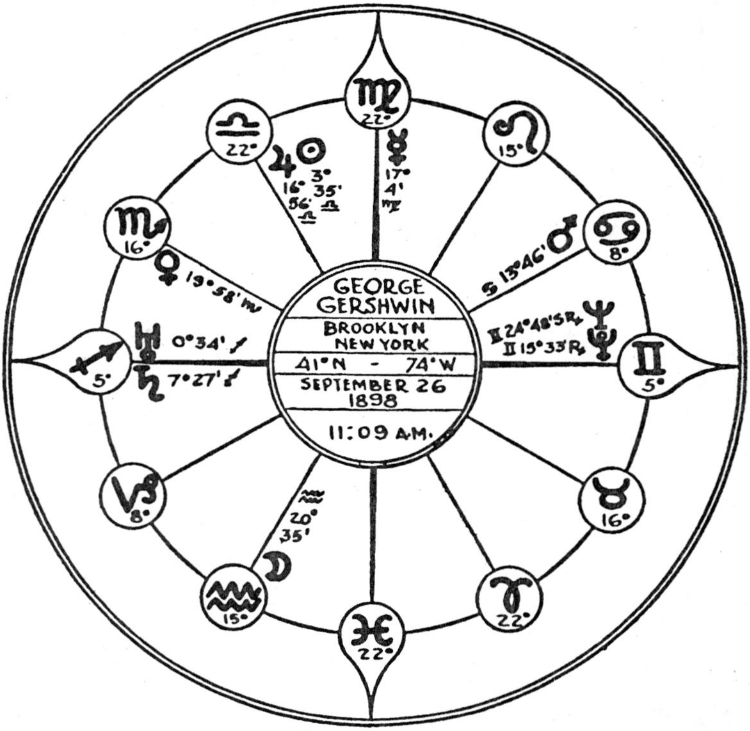

namic is less intellectually universal, or agonizingly imbued with the necessity for prophesying, than is the case with Upton Sinclair, whose exceptional concentration of planets in earth signs leads him to take a broom to the cosmos. Gershwin has a cosmic cross similar to Sinclair's, but his point of stimulus emphasizes his art for its own sake, while the crusading author is led from people to issues and from broad sympathy to wild utopianism by his focal moon. Gershwin's energies are more creatively directed or self-established than the efforts of Cecil Rhodes, and in consequence are devoid of all political economic stirrings. These men have the same T cross, but the point of stimulus for Gershwin is personal and direct through Mercury, and for Rhodes is social and remote through Neptune.

Chapter Four

THE BOWL TYPE

When the planets lie to one side of the zodiac, dividing the circle in halves, they create one of the simplest of all possible patterns. This can happen anywhere among the signs, but in the case where the division corresponds to the main axes of the houses, the horizon and the meridian, the additional distinction establishes a hemisphere emphasis, one of the most useful of all focal determinators. The basis of the distinction in hemisphere emphasis, as well as in the other half-zodiac concentrations which are at least equally common, is a special type of conscious selfhood. This marks the *bowl* type of temperament. Fundamentally it is an extreme self-containment. A bowl holds things, and a *bowl* individual is one who always has something to bear.

The *splash* type is universal, an individual capable of wide impersonal organization as well as broad prodigality. The *bundle* type is universal in a reverse sense, subconsciously self-mobilized or intent, and at his best a trailblazer, exactly as he is very selfish at his worst. The *locomotive* type is the dynamic executive, either an efficient co-ordinator or a ruthless, roughshod self-seeker. These pattern-types have all been derived from a whole-analysis of the zodiacal circle, recognizing a distribution of the self out of a working together of all the factors in the native's environment. Beginning with the *locomotive* type, however, the dynamic drive of an individual's life has its source in the relationship set up between an occupied and an unoccupied section of the zodiac, and this introduces a new factor in the make-up of human temperament. Starting with the *bowl* type, the whole dynamic of man, his total power of achievement, arises in his instinctive realization that he is set off against a definite part of the world, that there is a complete segment of experience from which he is excluded in some subtle fashion. The *bowl* not only holds something, but also places whatever it holds into relationship with a larger consideration.

The occupied segment of the bowl horoscope reveals the activity and organization of the self, since planets are significant according to their place by sign and house, and the unoccupied segment becomes a challenge to existence, or the need and emptiness to which the native must direct his attention. The outstanding characteristic of the *bowl* temperament is its marked sense of what is self-contained in contrast with what the self cannot hold, and this takes an everyday form in an advocacy of some cause, the furtherance of a mission, an introspective concern over the purpose of experience. The *bowl* native always has something to give to his fellows, whether literally or psychologically, whether constructively or vindictively, because his orientation to the world arises from division; that is, frustration and uncertainty. The leading planet, determined in exactly the same way as for the *locomotive* pattern, gives a point of application, and shows where and how the native seeks to carry out his mission or gain his everyday justification for existence.

The leading planet is of secondary importance in the *bowl* pattern, unless it is found in a strong opposition or cosmic cross. The fundamental attack on the problems of life by the *bowl* individual is indicated more significantly by the tilt or house-position of the bowl-segment. This corresponds to the relation of the empty trine to the angles in the *locomotive* type, a point of secondary importance in that pattern. While the former temperament is more functional in its forms of interest, really more concerned over the how than the what of its activity, the *bowl* character is more definitely self-expending, or self-seeking, and more practically interested in what things mean and what they are. It continually throws the emphasis from the signs into the houses. In a general way the *bowl* tends to "scoop up" things and initiate experience when the position of the leading planet ranges from the fourth cusp, up and over the ascendant, to the midheaven cusp, and then inclines to "capture" things or consummate various phases of life when the leading planet is placed similarly from the tenth angle down over the descendant to the nadir.

The *bowl* type has a convenient and outstanding example in the horoscope of Oliver Cromwell.

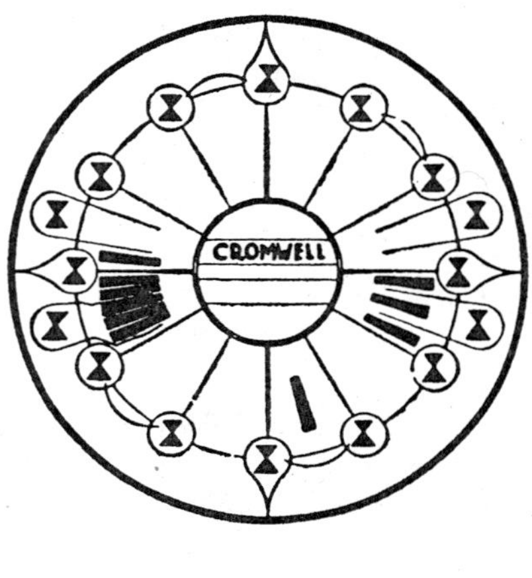

Here the planets are distributed through four houses and six signs, with a concentration of six planets on and around the ascendant. As a result the chart is not altogether ideal in its planetary spread, but is highly typical otherwise, and it identifies a valuable prophetic figure. The distribution is much better than appears to the eye, because only one sign is empty in the bowl area. The planets defining the pattern are in close opposition, participating in a T cross by fairly close orbs, with the result that the strength of the *bowl* here lies in the configuration rather than in the even spacing of these ten bodies. The leading planet is slightly above the horizon, but the chart is taken as a legitimate case of all planets below the earth since the time of day is not known within narrow limits, and especially since this hemisphere emphasis describes the life of the native with considerable accuracy. Thus his primary concern is in getting down a real foundation for life, and in reordering the basis of the society in which he finds himself. The tilt of the bowl in this particular hemisphere emphasis always gives the scooping activity, revealing a native who picks up or collects the materials of experience. It shows Cromwell's capacity for mobilizing and conserving the resources of a Puritan way of life. The horizontal position of the bowl is the only one that indicates pure conservation, or Cromwell's extreme skill in preserving the values for which he fought. Because the bowl's brim lies even, self-containment is most intense, most completely centered in the cause or sense of mission to which the native responds. This is the type of hemisphere emphasis found in the horoscope of Martin Luther.

Oliver Cromwell is the great prophet of the present Anglo-Saxon way of life, since his battle was not only for Protestantism and the Reformation, but also for the new sovereignty of man; which rests in Parliament as representative of the people at large, and not in the king's person. His prophetic influence continues in the living political, religious and cultural manifestation of man's self-responsibility.

Another example of the *bowl* type, as it falls away from the *bowl* ideal, is found in the horoscope of Frédéric Chopin.

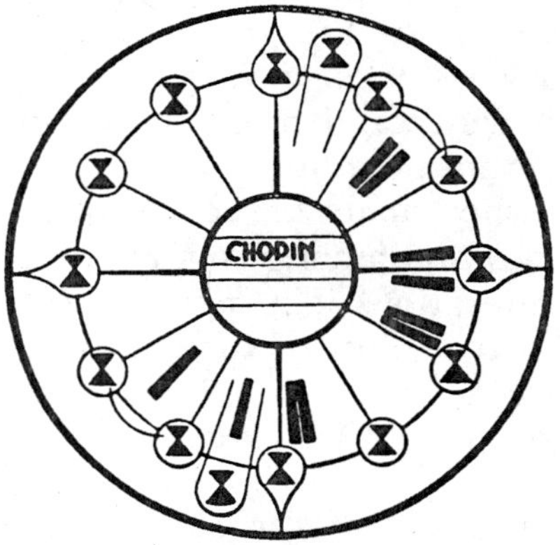

Here the distribution of the planets, in comparison with Cromwell's chart, is much closer to the ideal, since they are found in six houses and six signs, with only one house and one sign empty on the occupied side. The defining planets are only barely within orb of an opposition, however, and there is no T cross, so that the horoscope has a less general integrative strength, despite its closer approach to the ideal pattern. The span of planets exceeds the half of the wheel by twelve degrees, but this is not enough deviation to invalidate the classification. The lack of hemisphere emphasis identifies a life of greater functional or creative potentiality, but one less apt to be significant in everyday or conventional circumstances. The tilt of the bowl is again of the scooping order, so that the self-centering interest of Chopin was initiative. The sense of mission in his life, his effort for the cause of music, was instrumented by his demand, as prerequisite to composition, that everyone around him cater to the self-indulgence through which alone he could call upon his creative powers.

Chopin is a prophet of the romantic spirit in music, carrying the genius of the Enlightenment into his chosen art. Other figures have since taken up this prophetic mantle, to give much wider and more significant application to that freedom from mere form which Chopin represented, but the man who "made music out of discord" holds his own unique position among composers. His life was a supreme exemplification of a capacity to maintain a calm insouciance in the midst of turmoil, at least through the intervals between his own tantrums, or to demonstrate the full self-containment of his pattern in everyday experience.

A further example of the *bowl* type, as it falls away from the *bowl* ideal, is found in the horoscope of Benjamin Disraeli.

Here the distribution of the planets is fairly even through the houses, without an unoccupied one in the span of seven, but in the signs the spread is more ragged, with two of them empty. There is an added problem in this chart because, of the planets which define the *bowl*, the one in the third house is Pluto, and it was undiscovered in Disraeli's own lifetime. With this planet removed, the bowl has too short a span; with it in place, too long. In the first instance classification under the *bundle* pattern

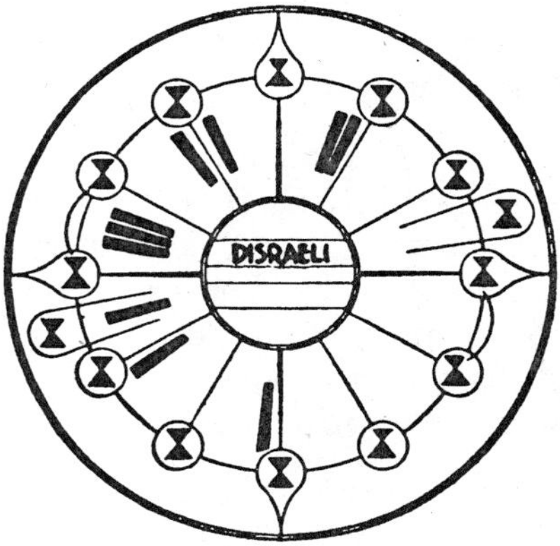

is possible. In the actual conditions of the native's personal life, or in his own generation, the interpretation of his horoscope would be well guided by such a typing. In the second instance, however, there is no possibility of identifying Disraeli's temperament by the *locomotive* pattern because there is no defining empty trine.

Benjamin Disraeli, Earl of Beaconsfield, is a prophet of the British Empire which he helped to put together in effective form. The significance of the events in English history after 1930, challenging his handiwork, is revealed importantly by the difference made by Pluto in this prophetic horoscope. Thus it is in its *bowl* resource, its power of self-containment, that Disraeli's structure of empire begins to regather its opportunity, and to remake its world in Pluto's era. The tilt of the bowl places the chart in the capturing category, indicating the power of recovery and completion. It is also narrowly close to a case of all planets east, or a horoscope in which a native's destiny rests entirely in his own hands, with a consequent tendency toward a healthy self-realization. Without Pluto, however, the approach is to a *bundle* pioneering, and a more primitive self-sufficiency.

Disraeli in his personal life was the dandy, poseur and self-seeker, but his skill in commandeering what he wanted, and in bringing it to bear usefully in meeting his needs, was a personal weakness which in his public life became a great strength. By climbing high in self-aggrandizement, he was able to make a prophetic contribution to his England in the political arena.

An example of the *bowl* type as it approaches the ideal extreme, among contemporary or near-contemporary figures, is found in the horoscope of Abraham Lincoln.

Here the planets are distributed fairly evenly through four houses and seven signs. While two houses are unoccupied, and are also adjacent, there are no empty signs in the bowl itself. There is no defining opposition, and no T cross to give strength to the pattern through a planetary configuration; however, all planets are above the earth, and this gives a strong circumstantial emphasis to the life. Indeed, the hemisphere emphasis reveals the extent to which Lincoln was compelled to lead an outer, practical and highly objective existence. He suffered his inner frustrations, and experienced his subjective deficiencies, in silence and by himself.

The house position of the bowl in this chart reveals a maximum self-emptying, in contrast to the brimfulness or self-certainty of temperament exhibited by Cromwell. This affords an insight into Lincoln's caution, or the agonizing uncertainty through which at times he suffered before making his decisive moves. In this upside-down horizontal emphasis there is the strong capturing procliv-

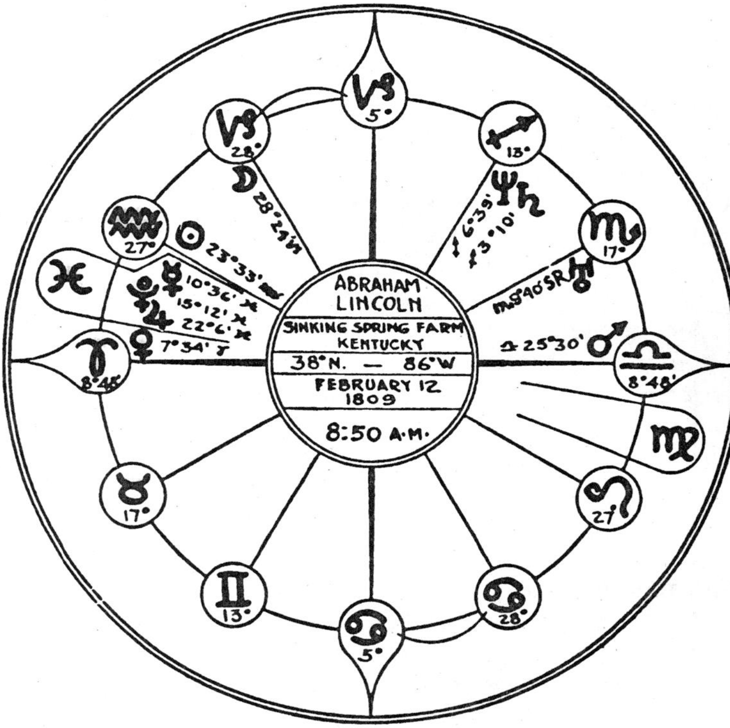

ity, but no power to retain any fruits of the efforts of self for the enjoyment of self. Lincoln may be compared with Queen Victoria in this connection, since her chart, of those given in the appendix, has the same hemisphere emphasis. Both the British queen and the American president had a gift for dramatizing the values of life in their own personalities. In some respects, this suggests a glass bowl put over a microscope, or wax flowers, the metaphorical goldfish bowl in which individual privacy is unknown. Lincoln is a prophet in the truest sense of the word. He had no real life on his own account at all.

The leading planet in the chart is Mars, duplicating the cases of both Cromwell and Disraeli. This reveals the pioneer drive in these lives, or the unusually sharp call to an active pacemaker's rôle in the careers of all three men. Lincoln's case demands a cause that can be embodied in his person, because of the south hemisphere-emphasis. He creates the immortal quality of his own life through his skill in recognizing and capturing elements of permanent value in the American political scene. His leading Mars, angular in a cardinal sign, holds him at the critical forefront of issues. He grew to manhood under difficult conditions. His early life was struggle, his romantic period a chronicle of frustration, his adult inner experience a chapter of unremitting suffering. The self-containment of the *bowl* type at its worst makes him a being apart from his fellows, misunderstood and beyond the possibility of real intimate companionship. But at its best it gives him unbelievable resources, and he found a prophetic happiness in carrying out the vision of his age. He met people and events with a mixture of humor and understanding which protected his own highly sensitive feelings, and enabled him to become the living embodiment of everything worthwhile in the nation's tradition.

The basic focal determinator is the hemisphere-emphasis above the earth, which is the outstanding feature of the horoscope and an adequate guide to its detailed interpretation. In addition, the chart is very exceptional in the fact that there are no major aspects between the two principal planets in any of the four departments into which planetary activity is divided. This means that Lincoln has

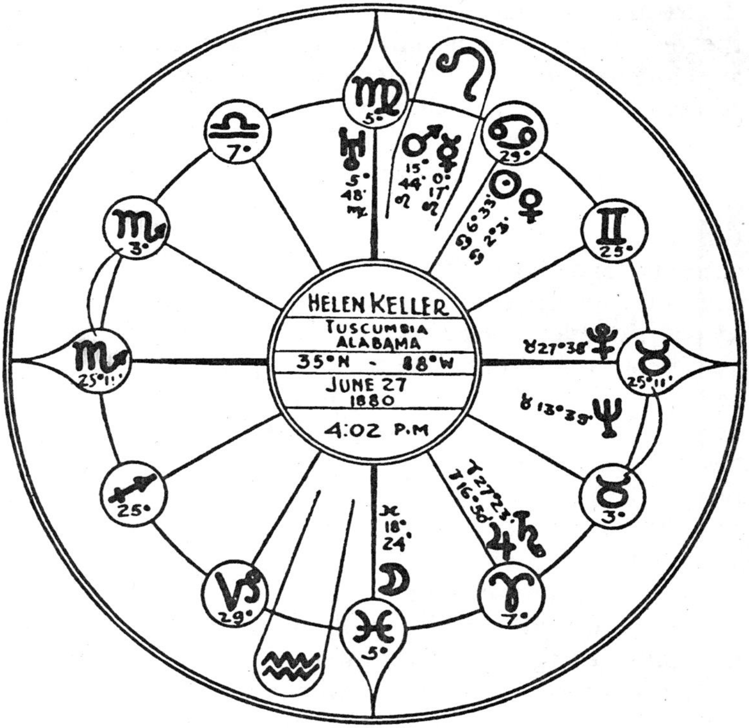

a limited capacity for integrating his actions, and that in consequence he is almost wholly dependent upon developments in the situation around him for uncovering his life pattern.

A second example of the *bowl* type among contemporary or near-contemporary figures, and an illustration of deviation from the ideal extreme, is found in the horoscope of Helen Keller.

Here the spacing of the planets is close to the ideal. There are no empty houses among the span of seven, and the one empty sign is hardly significant because planets are close to its cusps on either side. The bowl is also ideally coincident with the house axis, providing a striking case of all planets west. Since there is no T cross, and since the defining opposition is some minutes outside the widest orb of aspect allowed the moon in any normal situation, the horoscope comes under the general category of circumstantial or house rather than functional or sign emphasis. This shows that Miss Keller's life is largely conditioned by exterior events. Her career is prophetic in the same way as Lincoln's. He found himself by living the values of his age, and by embodying in himself the ideals of those around him. Her life differs, however, in the fact that she has a much higher power of free choice, under the emphasis of the midheaven over the horizon, although with the distinct limitations of a west hemisphere-emphasis. The western concentration links her with Woodrow Wilson, the data for whose chart is given in Appendix C. She is compelled to make the best of the affairs in which she finds herself, and her achievement must be centered in the increasing skill with which she learns to express herself in simple either-or experience.

Her leading planet is the moon, which shows that her achievement must be public in nature, and that it must be rooted in her sympathy with the affairs of men and women generally. Her life affords an exceptional illustration of the *bowl* type's weakness and strength under the most adverse of possible situations. Stricken in infancy with the loss of sight, hearing and smell, and rendered mute in consequence, her handicap demonstrated the complete limitation of the western emphasis. Public interest under the leading moon's influence, through the gifted Miss Sullivan and the Horace Mann School, opened the doors of hope for her. While the lack of air emphasis in the horoscope contributes to the possibility of sensory deficiency, it also emphasizes the need for contact with others as a justification for existence. This provides a dynamic for the task of building up a substitute set of sense-skills, enabling her to know the world and to meet its problems despite her limitation.

Helen Keller, as a prophet of real stature, reveals the practical extent to which man may go in conquering his environment, and in discovering his own potentialities, by his power of making choices. She dramatizes the principle, expressed by Jesus, that man is not born blind in order to suffer, or even be handicapped, but only that the "works of God may be made manifest", i.e., that the acting capacity of the human soul may be revealed. The individual who never knows restriction is never a prophet of life-mastery. The real question faced by the astrologer is not the degree of limitation put upon an individual by his circumstances, but rather the degree of use to which he may put his own experience. Helen Keller thus is far more free than the person who, with all his senses, does not have the "sense" to know his own bondage to inconsequential ideas, to his own lack of genuine self-realization.

Thus the fundamental purpose envisioned by modern astrology, in horoscope interpretation, is the indication of the effective employment to be made of facets of character, and aspects of its situation; so that conformity to limitation as such is unnecessary. No eventuality is presented as absolute, or beyond possibility of modification by free choice. This ethical principle has been generally accepted, for a century or more, in its original form as the dictum that the astrologer must "never predict death".

A third example of the *bowl* type among contemporary or near-contemporary figures, and an illustration of deviation from the ideal, is found in the horoscope of Abdul Baha.

Here the distribution of the planets is relatively even, with no empty houses and one empty sign in the bowl segment. While there is a close defining opposition, there is no really legitimate T cross, and the pointing of the chart is therefore circumstantial, as in the two preceding cases. However, there is no hemisphere emphasis either, to bring the house relations to a sharp focus in the issues of life, and in consequence there is some indefiniteness in the life direction. The tilt of the bowl gives the scooping or broadly self-starting temperament, and the leading planet is Saturn, indicating the native's depth of understanding, and revealing his basic spiritual interest.

Abdul Baha, better known to many by his real name, Abbas Effendi, was the outstanding leader of a definitely world-wide religion arising out of Mohammedanism. His Bahai movement places its emphasis on the unity of mankind, and on the common roots in all religious faith. He is the prophet who sought to live its demand for universality, and the concepts of Bahaism under his influences reflect the self-containment which characterizes the *bowl* pattern. The Saturn point of application in the horoscope of Bahaism's most effective exponent indicates the Bahai certainty of foundations. The focal determination in the chart is provided by the absence of emphasis in earth signs, which stimulates Abdul Baha's keen sense of the world's need for an increased concern over the practical and every-

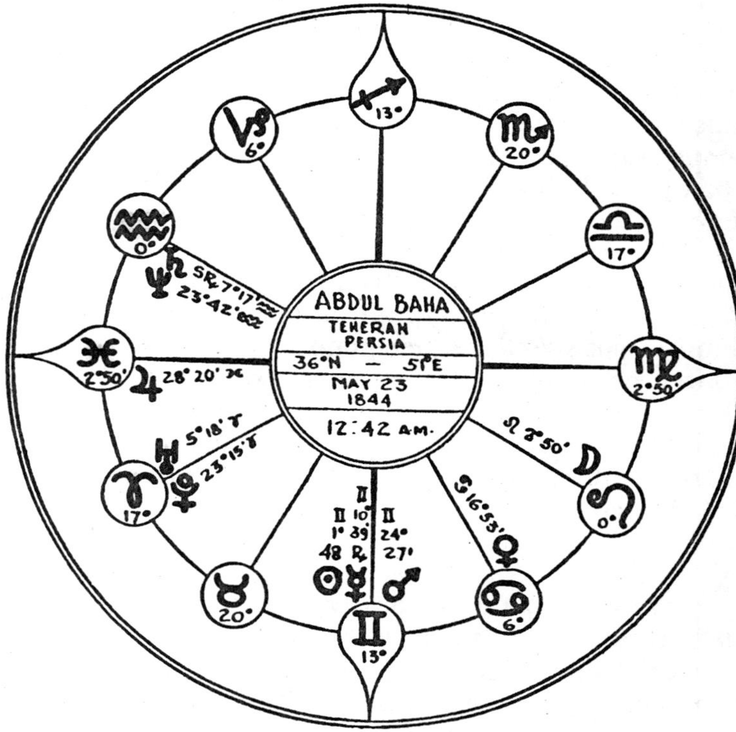

day relations and implications of experience. There is also a tendency of the planets to form pairs, not as marked as in the chart of Jeff Davis, but indicating Abdul Baha's instinct for doing things of importance, and affording vital guidance for the detailed analysis of his life.

A fourth example of the *bowl* type among contemporary or near-contemporary figures, and an illustration of deviation from the ideal extreme, is found in the horoscope of Edgar Allan Poe.

Here the distribution of the planets is somewhat uneven. No exact time of birth is known, and in consequence this is a solar chart, without real houses. There is only one empty sign, but the total span of the planets is shorter than the defining opposition by more than a sign. Therefore the figure is like that of William McKinley, in which the planetary span is greater by four degrees. Why is McKinley a *bundle*, and Poe a *bowl*? For one thing, the McKinley chart gains its extra span from Pluto, while Pluto is not significant here, and for another, McKinley's concentration of planets is central, while here the grouping is toward the bowl's rim, with a planetary emphasis which in every way suggests a hemisphere division rather than a confining-trine type of activity. It is impossible to know what the tilt of the bowl might be, but Mars is the leading planet in any case, showing the pioneer impulse.

Poe's self-containment took the destructive form marked in his dissipations, a factor which unquestionably shortened his life and diminished his usefulness, but it also equipped him with the same breadth of creative imagination which made Helen Keller's achievement possible. Poe was a critic of importance, the actual inventor of the modern detective story, and a poet who contributed immeasurably to the appreciation of words and their coloring. He became a prophet of great new potentials in literature. In his own actual consciousness he feels called on to throw his life into the cause of art, and in this he displays the fundamental *bowl* genius. The focal determinators of primary importance in the chart are the stellium in Pisces, and Jupiter as a singleton in disposi-

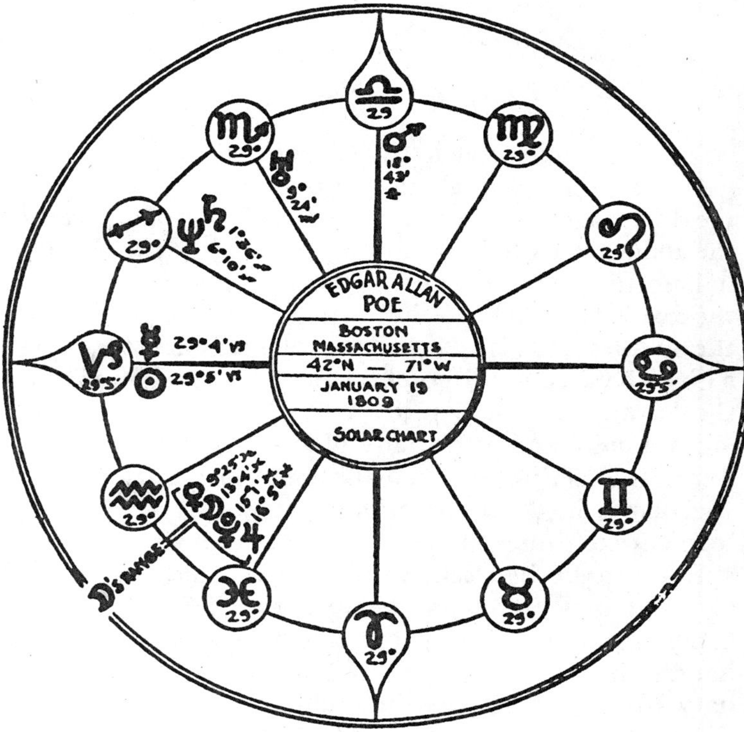

tion. The stellium will hold no matter at what time of day the birth took place, since the moon cannot possibly move out of the configuration. The grouping of the planets in Pisces reveals Poe's poetic appreciation, his emotional and humanistic depths, his power of discursive reasoning. Jupiter in disposing of all the other planets reveals his expansive power, and also the lack of any check upon the creative outpouring of his own consciousness.

Chapter Five

THE BUCKET TYPE

THE distinctions that have identified the temperament patterns so far have all been based upon regularity. The ideal has been an even distribution of the planets around the zodiac as a whole, or through one-third, two-thirds and half sections of the wheel. The next step is to recognize the patterns in the possible irregularities of a chart, and the simplest case is when all the planets except one are in a given half-section. In other words, the *bowl* type becomes the *bucket* when it acquires a "handle". The handle provides a new and important point of application in the horoscope, acting in much the same manner as the leading planet in the *locomotive* and *bowl* types. The bowl segment continues to mean just what it does when it constitutes a type by itself, so that its tilt and anything else about it may be considered profitably. Such details become secondary to the more important indication of the handle, however, and should be ignored in any preliminary analysis of a *bucket* individuality.

When the bowl's rim in the *bucket* pattern is coincident with the horizon or meridian, the "handle planet" is a singleton. This will occur in many cases, but not necessarily in any large number of them. The singleton is a focal determinator, indicating a special capacity or a gift for some particularly effective kind of activity. The handle planet, whether or not a singleton, reveals a characteristic and important direction of interest. The planets grouped in the segment opposite to the handle may approximate the *bundle* rather than the *bowl* pattern, but in such a case there is no suggestion of any modified *bundle* temperament, since the power of this *bucket* type lies in its functional linking of two given halves in the zodiac circle. It demands a single planet on one side, and nine on the other, because its meaning arises from this division, and from the consequent nozzlelike focus or release of energies. Thus two planets might constitute a handle if they were in an exact conjunction, but this may never be encountered. The bowl section is established by the handle, and not by any defining opposition or similar consideration.

A detail of importance in the *bucket* type is the position of the handle. When this is upright, or perpendicular to the bowl, the special direction of the energies is intensified, since there is an approximation to the fanhandle determinator. The bowl segment is always established in the position which creates a hemisphere emphasis if possible; otherwise it is taken with the handle as nearly vertical as the patterning permits. When the handle is situated clockwise through the zodiac, between the brim of the bowl and the vertical position, the life in general tends toward caution or self-conscious preparedness; when it lies between this vertical position and the other brim of the bowl, the life is more impulsive or inclined to respond to an immediate rather than future promise.

The *bucket* type indicates a particular and rather uncompromising direction in the life effort. The underlying interest in a cause which characterizes the *bowl* will be found, but with a much lesser concern over end-results, and with no basic desire to conserve either the self or its resources. An executive urge may seem much like the dynamic drive to action of the *locomotive* pattern. While a native under the *bowl* type may sacrifice everything for an ideal, one with a *bucket* horoscope is far more apt to adapt his allegiances to lines along which he can make his efforts count for the most. The *bucket* type at its best reveals the real instructor and inspirer of others, and at its worst the agitator and malcontent. In all cases it shows one who dips deeply into life, and who pours forth the materials of experience with unremitting zeal.

The *bucket* type has a convenient and outstanding illustration in the horoscope of Napoleon Bonaparte.

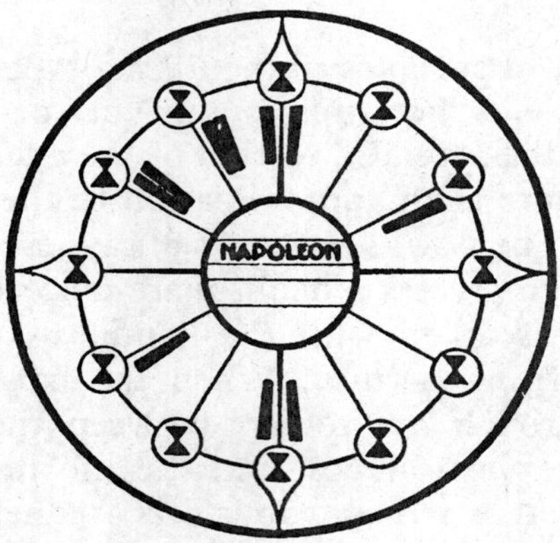

Here the distribution of the planets in the bowl segment is not as even as the ideal would indicate, since two empty houses are adjacent. However, the planetary spread by sign is better, because the two unoccupied signs are separated. The handle has not yet risen to the vertical position, giving Napoleon a temperament-set on the self-conserving side. This shows that he was defeated ultimately by over-caution rather than over-confidence. He moved to his downfall from apprehension, in the fear he might lose the initiative. His handle planet is Uranus, which was discovered in his boyhood, and it may be taken as a singleton, although not sharply defined as one, since the planets in the ninth and fourth houses are in the signs on the meridian axis. While he was highly responsive to the new order of civilization under Uranus, he leaned back on the old and outworn structures of kingly pomp and medieval splendor because of the west singleton, and thereby assured his own eclipse.

Napoleon remains an outstanding prophet of the new era in Europe. He broke down the crystallized ways of life in many different realms, and established many new foundations. The prophetic nature of his persisting achievements is revealed in the degree to which his figure has held the imagination of the modern world. He has embodied, in his own name and person, the ideal of the great leader who, by the sheer weight of his own personality and his sense of a task to be done, will lead humanity out of every morass of its own bungling.

Another example of the *bucket* type, as it falls away from the *bucket* ideal, is found in the horoscope of Dante Alighieri.

Here the planets are less even-spaced than in Napoleon's chart. The handle may be quite vertical, and ideal in that respect, but it is formed by Pluto. Moreover, Neptune completes the defining opposition of the bowl section, and forms the cosmic cross, perhaps by more than normally allowable orbs, to give focal determination to the chart. The new planets were undiscovered in Dante's time, and they alter the implication of the original horoscope very greatly. In his own age he was a *bowl* type, as his *Divine Comedy* well suggests. However, the consideration is not

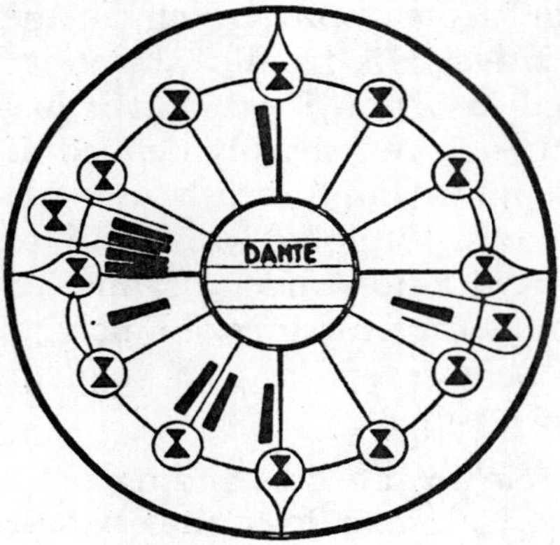

of the man but of his surviving influence, his contribution to the affairs of a modern world.

Dante lives in the hearts and minds of men as the prophet of medievalism. Until recently this has meant reaction, superstition and bigotry. Only a belated realization, that nineteenth-century science does not answer all the problems in life, has encouraged men to examine the earlier tradition with a more sympathetic understanding. Under the influence of Pluto, which puts this chart in the *bucket* pattern, Dante becomes the special spokesman in literary and religious realms for the vast, deep and hidden wisdom of the Middle Ages.

A further example of the *bucket* type, as it falls away from the *bucket* ideal, is found in the chart of George du Maurier.

Here a singleton planet opposes what otherwise would be a *bundle* pattern, but there is no fanhandle determinator, which would be the ideal case. The west singleton shows the compulsion which his environment exercises

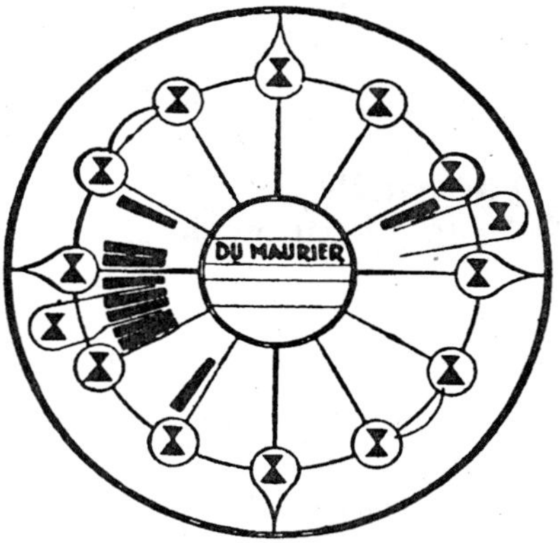

upon the native, marking his response to the social trends of his day. Saturn as the handle planet indicates his deep satirical skill, as well as the incisive pointing and psychological soundness of his fiction. The handle has not risen to the vertical position, so that his temperament leans to the conservative side, discouraging him from giving full rein to his creative talent.

George du Maurier is superficially a prophet of the power in pictorial propaganda. His work as an artist on *Punch* was directed to the task of influencing men by satire. However, he went beyond this and in his novels, *Peter Ibbetson* and *Trilby*, did pioneer work in awakening public appreciation for the occult, or for the deeper and unsuspected considerations of life. In his figure of Svengali he attains major prophetic stature, typifying magnificently the sinister efforts of modern men to rule their fellows by a basic manipulation of human thinking.

An example of the *bucket* type as it approaches the ideal extreme, among contemporary or near-contemporary figures, is found in the horoscope of William Jennings Bryan.

Here the spacing of the planets approximates the ideal with but one empty house and no unoccupied signs in the bowl segment. There is a defining opposition, but not the T cross which might have helped Bryan to a greater achievement. The handle has only risen to within a sign of the perpendicular position, and this makes him cautious, resulting in his loss of opportunity through hesitation or a sense of insecure possession of his own powers. Mars as the handle planet is also a west singleton. Bryan is a pioneer, because of this Mars influence, but under compulsion to express or amplify the ideas of others because of the western emphasis. He was a true prophet of the social unrest in the 1890's. He captured the leadership of the Democratic Party through his famous "cross of gold" speech, and held it for thirty years. Remaining an American prophetic symbol of utopianism, or the attempt to solve problems by panaceas, he reveals the *bucket* temperament superlatively. Like Napoleon, he would remake the world.

Bryan's life is significant in its relations of similarity and difference with other key personalities in the cultural transition. The parallel social function of William McKinley and Martin Luther, and the contrasting parallel between Luther and Bryan, have been indicated on page 40. The Luther-Bryan similarity is a different sort of distinction, astrologically and in life. Thus Uranus and the moon are, respectively, the rising and elevated planets in Bryan's chart, and they are equally emphasized as the confining planets of Luther's *bundle*. Uranus makes it possible, even for Luther in the sixteenth century, to voice the new cultural genius prophetically, and the moon gives both men their public. Both charts have a primary fire emphasis, and both individuals an intrinsic creativity.

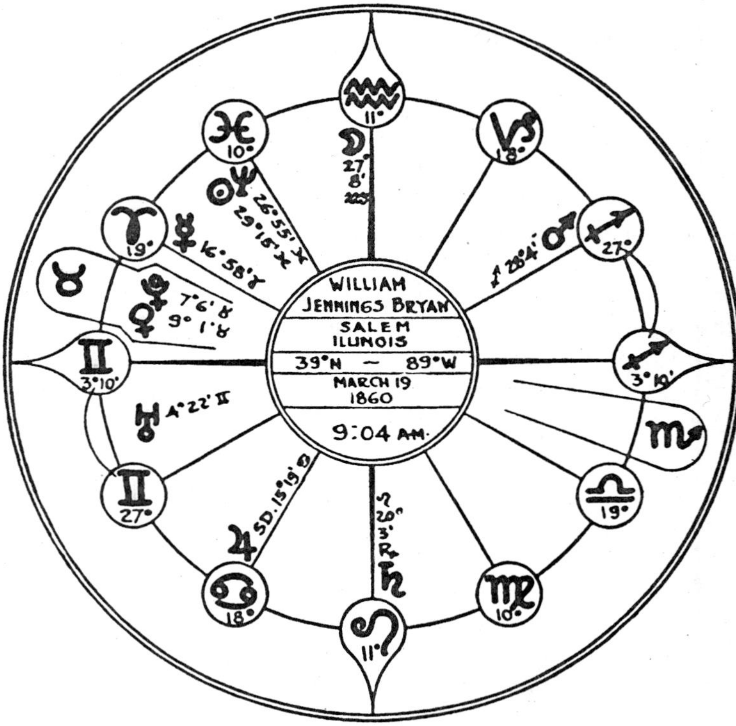

The focal determination of the chart lies primarily in the singleton Mars. A grand trine in fire signs, formed by wide orbs through a translation of light, gives Bryan his self-importance, and Mars sends him forth as a veritable Sir Lancelot, ready to slay or be slain.

A second example of the *bucket* type among contemporary or near-contemporary figures, and an illustration of deviation from the ideal extreme, is found in the horoscope of the famous astrologer, Evangeline Adams.

Here the planets are distributed somewhat irregularly through the bowl segment, yet there is only one empty sign with two unoccupied houses. The bowl has a defining opposition, participating in a fixed-sign T cross with Pluto as the point of stimulus. This emphasis of Pluto explains her continuing influence as the modern American prophet of astrology. Because the handle of the bucket has not risen to the perpendicular, Miss Adams like Bryan suffers from an inherent caution or an inability to put forth the whole content of her understanding. Saturn is the handle planet, and while not a singleton, giving her the critical powers of a Du Maurier, this planet yet endows her with a superb gift for seeing to the bottom of problems and digging deep in the analysis of a horoscope. Evangeline Adams is a prophet because astrology to her was not so much a profession as a cause, not so much a means for a professional success as an agency for expressing her conviction. Mars shows this as the leading planet of the bowl, identifying the secondary but strong pioneer drive, and the response of the public to her ground-breaking activities is revealed by the place of the moon in the defining opposition of the bowl segment. It is important to note how these additional factors supplement the type's basic indication. It is equally necessary to avoid confusion, failing to "see the wood for the trees" by employing too much detail for a preliminary whole-view. Miss Adams' case conveniently illustrates the significance of the "ring planets" in a *bundle* pattern.

The important focal determinator in this chart is Jupiter as a singleton in disposition, since the fixed cross becomes operative only in 1930. With Jupiter just above the

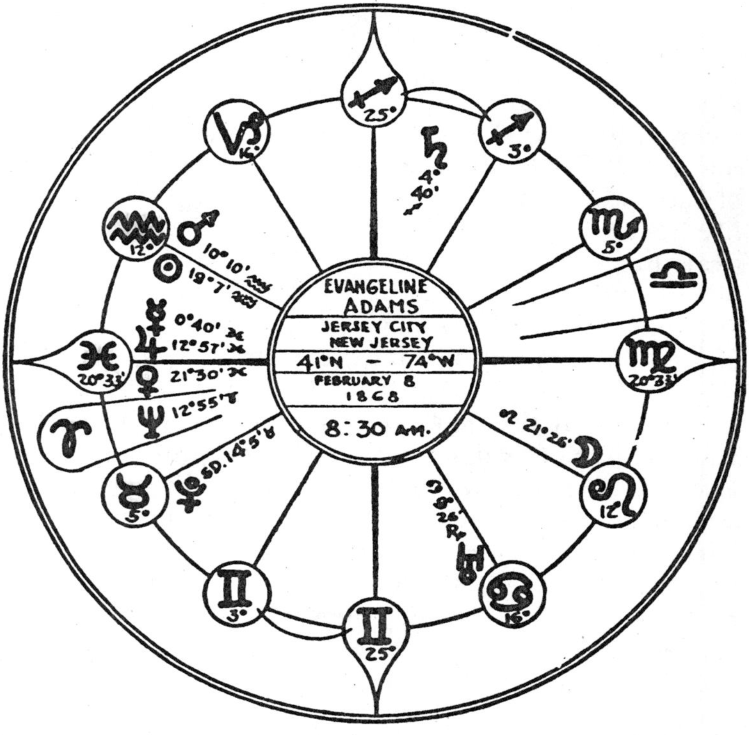

ascendant, which it rules, Miss Adams has the power to integrate her own capacities through a continual expansion of her own personality. She is able to make herself, under the emphasis of the twelfth house, a prophetic vehicle for much more than she suspects.

The third example of the *bucket* type among contemporary or near-contemporary figures, and an illustration of deviation from the ideal extreme, is found in the horoscope of Lewis Carroll (Charles Dodgson).

Here in detailed example is the type of chart already illustrated by the Du Maurier piano-key diagram, but a much more irregular case. The bowl apparently may be taken either north or east, with Saturn a singleton both south and west in any instance. The exceptional emphasis of Saturn shows that the whole functional pointing of the life lies in the direction of seeing the deeper side of practical things, Saturn singleton in the south, and also the deeper and more unsuspected compulsions under which everyone lives, Saturn singleton in the west. This emphasis of Saturn accounts for every subtlety to be found in *Alice in Wonderland*. Saturn as the handle planet is taken as south, with the bowl lying in the north, since otherwise the handle is not erect. It has not quite risen to the exact vertical position and this accounts for the native's diffidence even though the moon, as the leading planet in the bowl, catapults him into world-wide public recognition. Charles Dodgson wholly disappears in the prophet, or in Lewis Carroll as the immortal identity. His doubly-singleton Saturn is the voice of hidden potentiality, the promise to all men of an "under the surface" reality.

The focal determination, in addition to the singleton Saturn, is most importantly an absence of emphasis in water signs. This stirs Lewis Carroll to his intuition of a universality which he feels is lost to him, and perhaps to the whole world as well. He reached out for it in dry or barren fashion through his mathematics, but in a very alive and thrilling way through the world of imagination. Finding this universal note in a fellowship of rabbits and mice, caterpillars and playing cards, he gave his prophetic message to the world with the gentle and insinuating

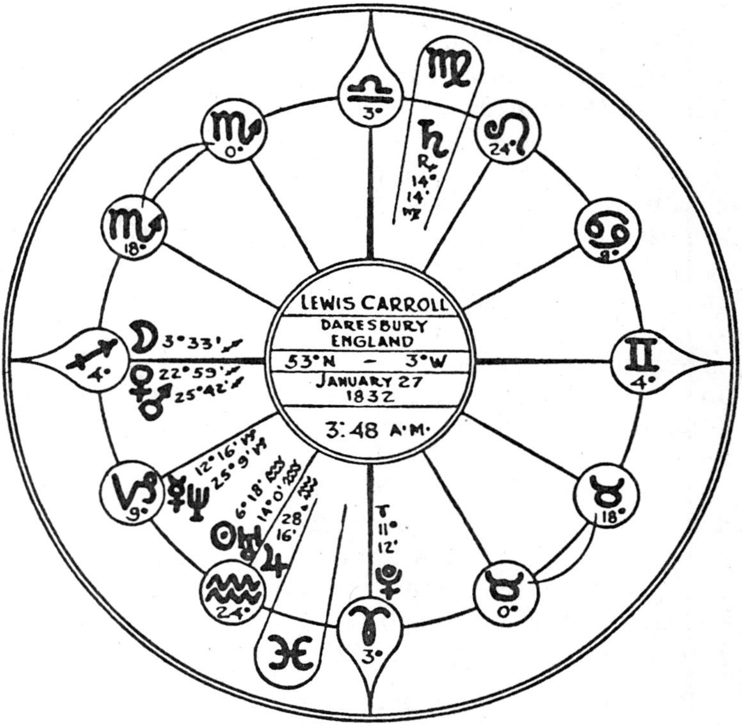

touch that the water triplicity might have developed. When he sought to be clever literally, and consciously, he was pitifully ineffective. When he took off the brakes of presumption, to give his deeper instincts full play under Saturn, his achievement was unsurpassed.

A fourth example of *bucket* type among contemporary or near-contemporary figures, and an illustration of deviation from the ideal extreme, is found in the horoscope of George Bernard Shaw.

Here again the bowl segment approaches a *bundle* cluster, and the grouping of the planets is quite irregular. The handle planet might be taken into a cardinal T cross by a translation of light, and it participates in another T cross formed across the lines of the signs, fixed and cardinal, and including Pluto, but these determinators are hardly sharp or regular enough for profitable preliminary consideration. The classification of the chart as *bucket* in type is suggested by the singleton Mars. Shaw thereby is revealed as primarily the pioneer, the protagonist for many diverse notions, the intellectual rebel of his age. Mars as a handle planet identifies his capacity to shift his interests, and indulge the experimentation so dear to his soul. Because the handle has risen and passed beyond the perpendicular, he is disclosed in his self-exhibition or in his flair for a free spilling of ideas and expending of energies. George Bernard Shaw is the prophet of genuine individuality. He encourages everyone who finds difficulty in casting off the censorship of society. He speaks for the intellectual freedom of the human soul.

The focal determination has its foundation in the sun as a singleton in disposition. This endows Shaw with his immense self-assurance, his capacity for believing himself rationally adequate to meet or discuss any issue. The singleton Mars instruments his self-realization superlatively. The emphasis of these two planets particularly indicative of leadership and initiative, added to the special pointing of self-resource which these two focal determinators reinforce in each other, is a dramatic illustration of the high-purposed specialization of the human temperament and its skills which, in a more general way, is always

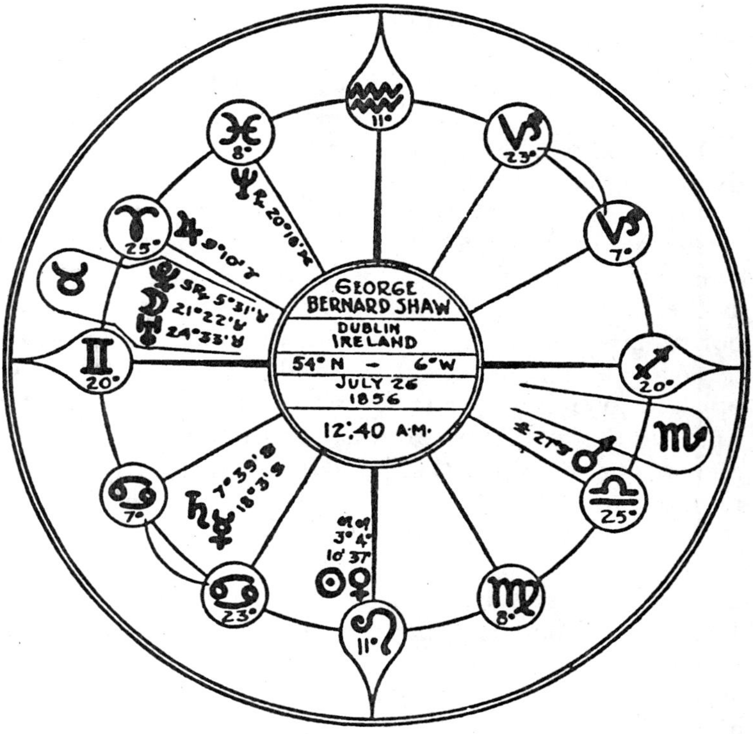

indicated by the *bucket* typing. This native is an unusual example of the uncompromising direction in life effort which, distinguished from the *bowl* typing, is concerned with the process rather than the purpose of living. Also he illustrates admirably the different type of intensity of character which distinguishes the *bucket* and the *bowl* types together from the more simple or primitive *bundle* set in temperament.

CHAPTER SIX

THE SEESAW TYPE

A SECOND basis for the recognition of patterns, through the irregular rather than the regular distribution of planets around the zodiac, lies in the symmetry of their clustering in any two groups roughly opposed to each other across the circle. The *bucket* type has been identified as the case where one planet, in one half-section of the horoscope, is opposite the nine in the other half, and the *seesaw* type may be described as the case where two are opposed to eight, three to seven, four to six or five to five in a similar emphasis of the half-sections or bowl segments. The ideal situation prevails when the arrangement of the two groups is most symmetrical, irrespective of the number of planets in each; or when the pattern is unmistakably obvious. The difficulty in borderline cases is to distinguish the *seesaw* properly from the *splash* and *locomotive* types. This pattern ideally will have two symmetrically opposite empty segments of at least a square-aspect span each. These two unoccupied sections must always be present, and they must lie on the line of direct opposition enough to define the distinct half-sections in the chart. Neither of the empty segments should be less than a sextile's span, and only one should be that narrow in any special case where the planetary groupings are not directly opposite each other.

The *seesaw* pattern describes a temperament-set which is essentially a further refinement of the *bucket* personality. It reveals a less-sharpened but much more definite balancing of life emphases at opposing or contrasting points in experience. It is a persistent move to a balance which is apt to give a characteristic rhythm, and this can be somewhat over-literally expressed in the figure of a teeter-totter. The indication is not so much an uncertainty of action, or reaction, as a tendency to act at all times under a consideration of opposing views or through a sensitiveness to contrasting and antagonistic possibilities. The *seesaw* temperament has its existence in a world of conflicts, of definite polarities. It is capable of unique achievement, through a development of unsuspected relations in life, but it is also apt to waste its energies through its improper alignment with various situations.

It is not always possible to identify a planet as the point of application in the *seesaw* type. However, the chart is more dynamic, and the chances for an easy and objective success are greater, when a planet is made focal by the typing. The axis of the two groups is defined by a straight line which passes through the center of the zodiac circle, and most nearly marks the midpoint in each of the planetary aggregates. It describes the point of application at its end primarily emphasized by some focal determinator. If no such emphasis is present, the life tends to be significant at the side of the greater number of planets, or sometimes where they are concentrated most closely.

The *seesaw* type has a convenient and outstanding illustration in the horoscope of Percy Bysshe Shelley.

Here three planets are opposed to seven, and the general symmetry is exceptional, contributing to the poet's gift of rounded expression and revealing his skill in delineating the outlines of beauty in experience. The

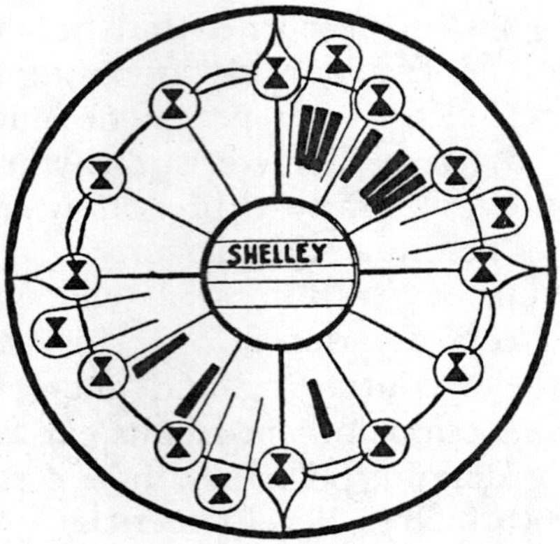

point of application in the chart is created by the planetary opposition close to the cusps of the ninth and third houses, established at the southwestern pole of the axis by the preponderant weight of the planets there. Thus the dynamic drive of Shelley's life lies in the eighth house, identifying the process of regeneration as central in all his understanding, and through all his personal struggles. There is also, in confirmation, an emphasis on the capping or consummating function of experience through the position of the seesaw axis, which reveals the application of the life's energies in the same way as the defining opposition or rim in the *bowl* type.

Percy Bysshe Shelley is a remarkable leader in the anti-intellectualism of the romantic movement, a prophet of free experience or of an unbound Promethean employment of the human mind and its instinctive powers. A passionate rebel in his own day, he possessed the courage if not the means for living the daring conceptions that sprang to vivid reality within his own comprehension.

He died in the belief that the world had failed to understand his message, and that the rejection was final. He was a prophet in the Biblical tradition, believing that the way to awaken men was to outrage their sensibilities. He was an alien among his fellows from boyhood, and because they could not appreciate him, they paid no attention to what he said. His career was spectacular, however, and many have come to hail him as the messiah of the new age and of a true social reform. These sharp lines of conflict and contrast in his temperament-set make him pre-eminently. the archetype of the *seesaw* pattern.

Another example of the *seesaw* type, as it falls away from the *seesaw* ideal, is found in the horoscope of Emanuel Swedenborg.

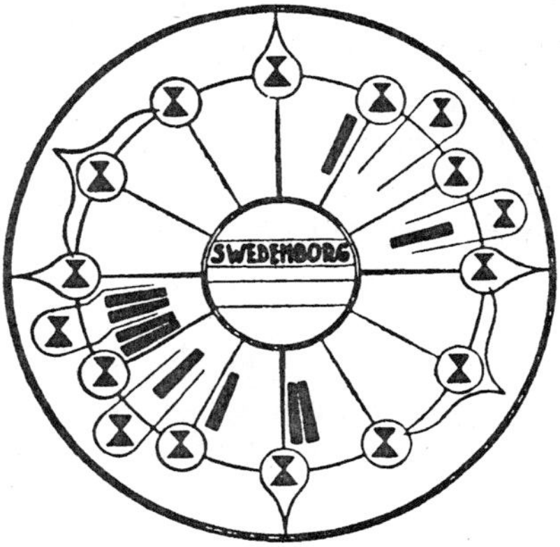

Here two planets are opposed to eight, and the arrangement approximates the ideal symmetry, and indicates the rounded genius of the Swedish scientist. Because the pattern of his chart, in contrast with that of Shelley, is much more modified by the position of the three planets of recent discovery, none of them active in his lifetime, the consideration turns far more on the surviving influence of the man than on the significance of his life in his own age. While a study of the effect of events on his development would be interesting, it is virtually impossible in any long perspective of history. What is presented in any notable nativity out of the past is its contribution to the present, as an example case if in no other way. The point of application in this horoscope is established in the ninth-house planet, by its weight as a singleton in Swedenborg's own lifetime, and it reveals the intellectual or ninth-house emphasis in his career.

Swedenborg has a direct prophetic function as the author of the revelations on which the Church of the New Jerusalem is founded, and a greater importance, not yet adequately appreciated, as a brilliant pioneer in modern science. Even more vitally, however, he is the outstanding prophet of a real spiritism. He could not be dismissed as a charlatan in his own day because he was widely acknowledged as the leading scientist of Europe. The point is not that his fame led people to take his word for things, but rather that it compelled more than usual attention for his activities. This produced a degree of unimpeachable evidence which would have been impossible for one of a lesser prophetic stamp to provide. The breadth of his interests illustrates the *seesaw* temperament in its exceptional reaction to opposing points of view and conflicting opportunities.

A further example of the *seesaw* type, as it falls away from the *seesaw* ideal, is found in the horoscope of Rudyard Kipling.

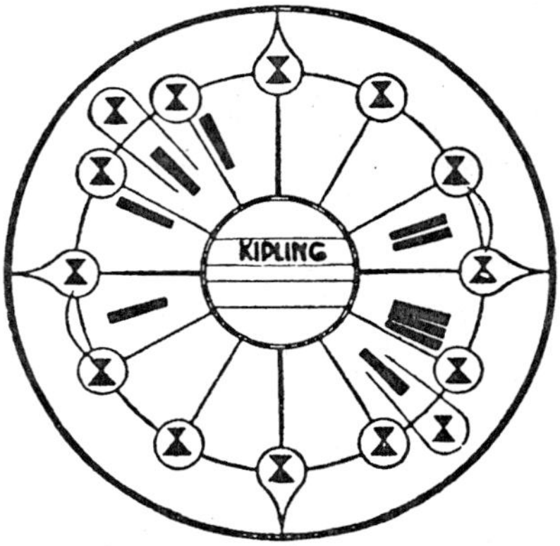

Here four planets are opposed to six, with considerable symmetry. The axis line of the seesaw is defined by the miniature fanhandle in the twelfth and sixth houses, and the point of application is therefore established in the first of these. The planet is the moon, which shows Kipling's necessarily public work, together with his striking gift under the twelfth house influence for bringing out the hidden motives and inner sensibilities of men and their affairs.

Rudyard Kipling is the great modern prophet of the East to the West, and also to a lesser extent of the Occident to the Oriental mind. While he affirmed, in his "Ballad of East and West" that "never the twain shall meet", he himself accomplished this very thing through his writings, in the simple terms of everyday living. He provides an excellent example of the mediating function found in the *seesaw* type. He drew geographic areas together in the same way that Swedenborg linked the invisible to the visible with a new pertinence, and that Shelley brought many thinkers to realize the value of the irrational as a check upon modern intellectual egotism.

An example of the *seesaw* type as it approaches the ideal extreme, among contemporary or near-contemporary figures, is found in the chart of Karl Marx.

Here three planets are opposed to seven. Because the arrangement is not very symmetrical, the chart indicates no particularly rounded-out competency in the native's case, and Marx, possibly as important as any single individual in nineteenth-century history, was almost totally irresponsible in his own personal life and affairs. The lack of symmetry might possibly suggest classification in the *bucket* type, but the empty sextile between Jupiter and Saturn, together with the fact that Mars as a handle planet would have little vertical position, suggests the present identification. The nearest approach to an axis emphasis in the Marx seesaw, since the asymmetrical placing of the two groups provides no midline as a basis of reference, is found in the position of Mercury opposing Uranus and Neptune by sign, although not by definite aspect. The validity of this axis in the horoscope is confirmed by the exceptional way in which Neptune's discovery coincides with the 1848 revolutions in Europe, marking an important point in Marx's impact on his own age, exactly as Uranus was discovered almost at the precise moment of revolution in the American colonies. Mercury's mundane opposition brings these factors to a focal point in the native's thinking.

Karl Marx is the prophet of revolution *per se,* and his living influence after his death is far more potent than anything centered in his own person. He is the author of economic doctrines which are transforming the world not only directly wherever his philosophy has government

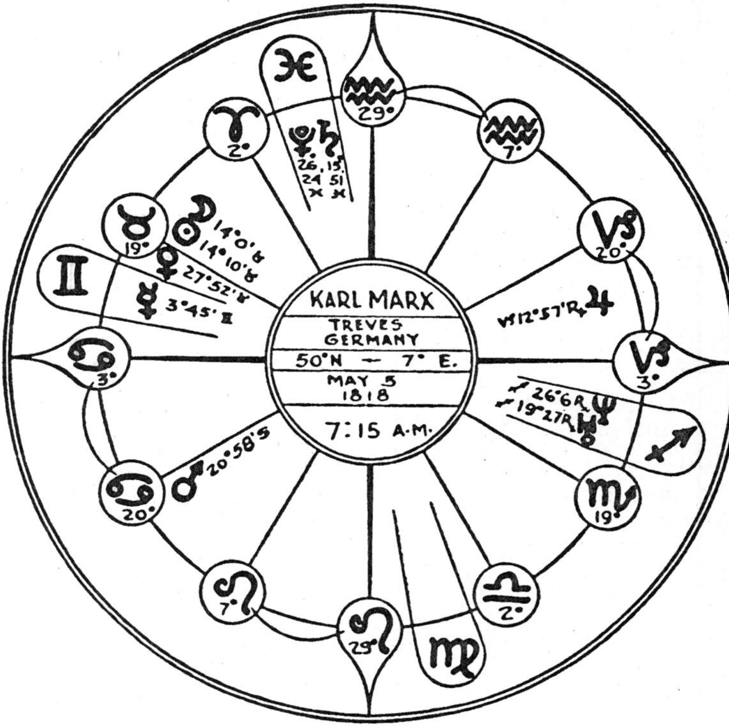

sanction, but indirectly in their influence on the whole world's economic structure. The focal determination in his horoscope is provided by the tendency of the planets to aggregate in pairs. Although this is not as marked as in the case of Jeff Davis, or even Abdul Baha, it is greatly accentuated by the almost exact conjunction of the sun and moon, and the less close but same relation of Uranus and Neptune. These conjunctions of two out of the four departmental pairs among the planets are a clue to his real integration as an instrument of the age in which he functioned, indicating that his social innocence was merely the sharpening of his life in the light of broader conflicts and contrasts in human affairs.

The second example of the *seesaw* pattern among contemporary or near-contemporary figures, and an illustration of deviation from the ideal extreme is found in the horoscope of Oscar Wilde.

Here four planets are opposed to six in a rather exceptional example of symmetry, reflected in the aesthetic refinement of the native and in his gift for a genuine rounded analysis of life. The axis of the pattern is provided by the actual opposition of Venus to three planets in a miniature fanhandle, with the point of application falling at the third house position. Venus in Scorpio as the significant planet accounts for the aesthetic finish in Wilde's writing. Scorpio with its general rulership over sexual functions gives some intimation of the weakness which brought him to ultimate disgrace. The position of Venus as the leading planet in the seesaw axis shows his life-activity to be of the scooping type, an interest in mobilizing experience, and also reveals his self-indulgence as a primary dynamic. Wilde persists in men's memory as a prophet for the artistic way of life, and his work is prophetic through its refinement of technique and subtlety.

The focal determination in the chart is provided by the grand trine in water signs. This is quite strong, indicating Wilde's universal consciousness, and also suggesting the unrestrained emotional self-indulgence at the root of his self-destruction. Venus, thanks to the miniature fanhandle, is focal in the grand trine as well as in the temperament-set pattern, and the inexorable quality in

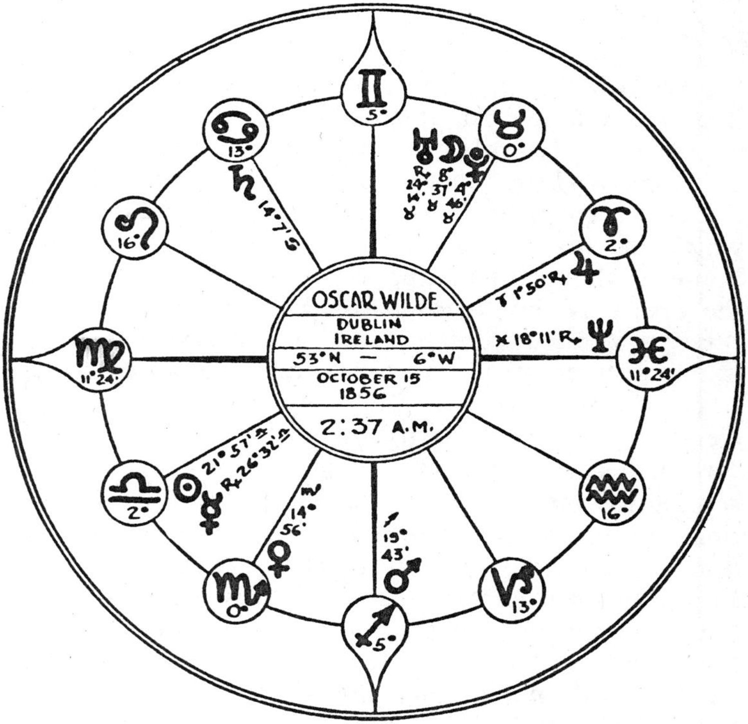

this planet's activity leads Wilde on blindly to the tragic end, once he has enshrined the abnormal. Like Shelley, he sought to increase his influence by outraging people, but he was unsuccessful because he lost all touch with ordinary emotions in his attempt to achieve universality by extraordinary means.

A third example of the *seesaw* type among contemporary or near-contemporary figures, and an illustration of deviation from the ideal extreme, is found in the chart of Luther Burbank.

Here two planets are opposed to eight, and the pattern is quite asymmetrical. It affords a particular illustration of the *bundle* type of aggregation as it becomes, in a sense, the nucleus for a different form of grouping. The axis of the chart is provided by another miniature fanhandle, which in this case establishes the moon in the ninth house as the point of application. The house identifies the primarily theoretical basis of the native's work, and the sign Virgo in containing the moon reveals his power of readjustment or his gift for testing a theory by practical trial-and-error methods. The moon itself, which is the elevated planet in the chart, shows not only the public nature of his work but also the great general appreciation coming to him as the result of his efforts. The axial position of the moon, only just past the meridian, indicates that his basic activity is always at a first or original stage in a capping or establishment of values. Luther Burbank is the prophet of man's ever-continuing conquest of nature. He was able to create almost any kind of growing plant at will, and become the outstanding mediator between the natural and the cultivated organism.

The focal determinator in this chart is the T cross in fixed signs. This is only effective through a translation of light, but it is important because it links Burbank's response to ever-practical considerations, as this is shown by his close square of Venus and Mars, with his intuitive and detached capacity for understanding relevant causes and manipulating them to his own ends, shown in turn by the specially subjective influence of a retrograde and cadent Jupiter in the ninth house. Venus, as the point of

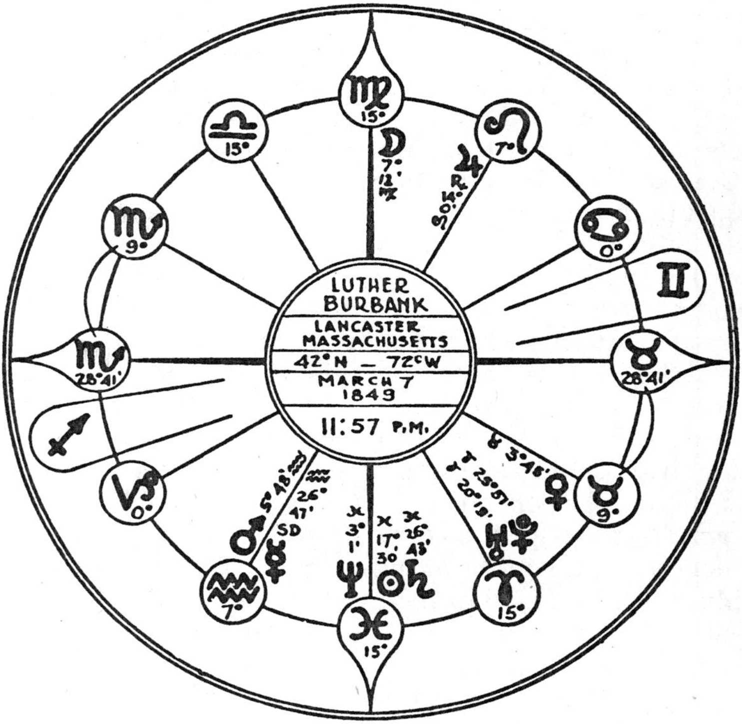

stimulus in this cross, reveals Burbank's particular capacity for bringing things to a conclusion, and for handling problems without compromise.

A fourth example of the *seesaw* type among contemporary or near-contemporary figures, and an illustration of deviation from the ideal extreme, is found in the horoscope of Paul von Hindenburg.

Here five planets are placed against five in an asymmetrical relationship which despite an empty trine is classified more effectively as a *seesaw* than a *locomotive* case. The only possible axis is formed by the planets on the Aries-Libra line. They constituted a miniature fan-handle prior to the discovery of Pluto, and there is no doubt but that Hindenburg definitely expressed his Uranus as his point of application up to that date. Subsequently he reacted more to the weight of the planets on the other side, and contributed to the rise of Adolf Hitler under Libra's less sharpened emphasis, its willingness to compromise. The example is valuable in showing the *seesaw* pattern at its point of greatest inertness, or as it exhibits too easy a temporizing in its five against five planets. This contributes to distinct deficiencies in dynamic drive unless the native renders a positive service to society as a functioning compensation. Von Hindenburg is the prophet of modern military efficiency, but he also represents the spirit of the old order making its tragically ineffective attempt to meet the issues of a new world. His blunt manifestation of his Uranus stood in the way of his early military career, but it expressed an actual seesaw genius, and his competency still brought him his chance in the first World War. His service to the German people, however, as president of the Weimar Republic, was merely a contribution of personal prestige in his futile effort to balance a situation of unresolved conflict.

The focal determination of the chart is found in the exceptionally strong cardinal T cross, with its point of stimulus in Jupiter. There is a cardinal predominance in addition to this, with seven planets in the quadrature. These factors indicate his superb temperamental equipment for meeting issues, for handling many vital and

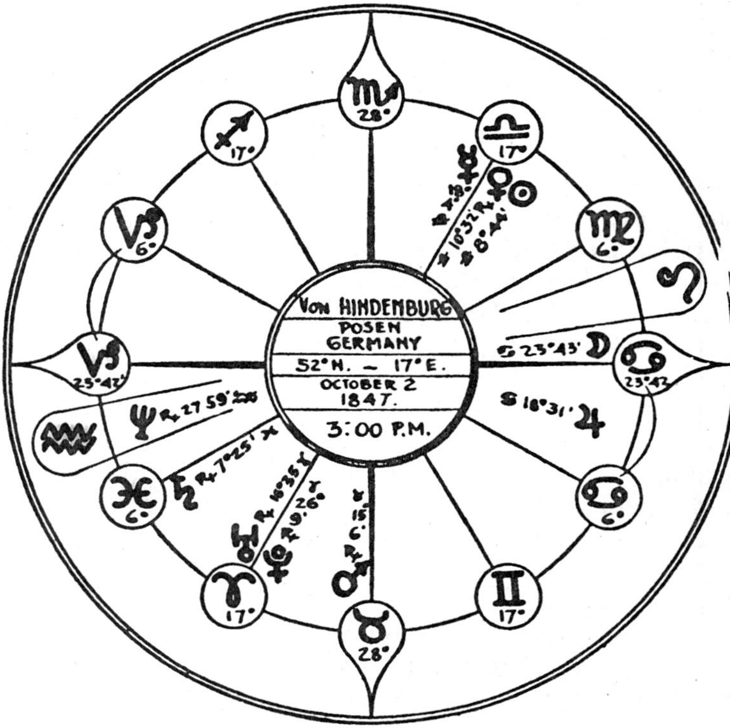

immediate problems. It is the chart of one who is at his best in an emergency, but who lives at his worst when life becomes no more than a task of carrying on under normal circumstances. The focal-determinator emphasis of Jupiter gives Hindenburg the co-ordinating or expansive power by which he achieves his military victories, but it leads him to count upon the weight of personality rather than effort when he faces a static situation.

Chapter Seven

THE SPLAY TYPE

THE planetary patterns introduced so far have been identified either on the basis of their even spread through the whole or some given part of the zodiac, or else on the basis of a recognizable symmetry when their grouping is definitely uneven. What remains is the case when the arrangement is neither even nor symmetrical. This would define the *splay* type, in the most simple terms, as anything left over from the other classifications, or as the pattern which cannot be recognized successfully as something else. To place a horoscope in the *splay* category would be a useless gesture, however, if the planetary arrangement had no positive meaning. The significance of the *splay* type comes from the fact that, in its ideal form, it reveals strong and sharp aggregations of the planets at irregular points. This suggests highly individual or purposeful emphases in the life, where the temperament juts out into experience according to its own very special tastes. The type is splay because it makes its own anchorage in existence; and also because the character of a native in this classification is marked by his rugged resistance to pigeonholing, either in the neat conventional compartments of nature, or in the idea-pockets of his associates.

The *splay* pattern represents a third fundamental concept in the classifications. In addition to even distribution, and to symmetrical aggregation, it reveals the idea of persistent emphasis on individuality. The *splay* chart has a varying number of points of application, set up on the rays or special spokelike emphases of the planetary groupings. These usually seem to lie more or less at random in the signs and houses, and to give a definite stance in the horoscope. They are like tripod feet, endowing the native with a splayfoot certainty in every approach he makes to the problems of life. Like the *splash* and *bundle* patterns, the *splay* group offers no preliminary technique for determining the most important planet in a chart, but instead reveals a very intensive personality who cannot be limited to any single steady point of application. He has a temperament inclined to be particular and impersonal in its interests, in contrast with the universal-impersonal set of the *splash* and the particular-personal set of the *bundle* types.

The *splay* type has a convenient and outstanding illustration in the horoscope of Henry VIII.

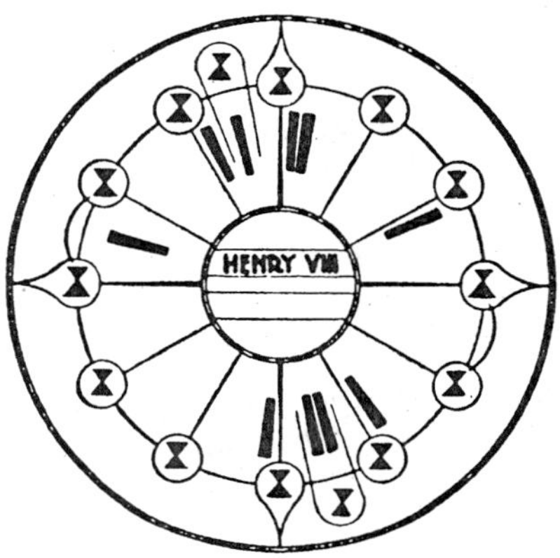

Here a classification under the *splash* type might seem more justified than in the case, for example, of Richard

Wagner, whose chart appears on page 16. However, the span between the two planets which embrace the northeast quarter, in both charts, is broader than a square here, and only three degrees more than a sextile there. The presence of an empty space even as great as a square is not an impossibility under the *splash* classification, as may be seen in the horoscope of Leon Trotsky on page 21. Trotsky is placed in the *splash* grouping because his planets have an exceptionally even spacing in general, because the one point of particular planetary aggregation in Taurus involves the recently discovered Neptune and Pluto, and because the division of the planets into groups of five and five is the over-symmetry which always tends to fall away into the *splash* temperament. A *seesaw* classification for Henry VIII is entirely possible, but the single planets in his seventh and twelfth houses stand apart from the midheaven cluster in a definite symmetry which indicates more than the simple teeter-totter temperament, and so must be taken as a true *splay* arrangement.

Henry VIII is the prophet of political expediency, and his opportunism, exhibited in many different realms, demonstrates the real genius of the *splay* type. His ecclesiastical accomplishments which, alone of his works, are known to the average layman, resulted from his extraordinarily clever course more or less midway between the Protestants and Catholics, avoiding an internal disunity which might have been fatal to England. He was successful in countering the political moves of his famous and able contemporary, Charles V. He kept events fluid enough so that his home affairs could be put in order, and the English economy given a chance to brace itself for the inevitable conflict. Thus he laid the foundations for a real British navy. While an egotistical Tudor with an almost drunken mania for power, he yet encouraged the arts, furthered the great fifteenth-century recrudescence, and endowed his country with the heritage seen in its flowering under Elizabeth and James. His varied gifts are indicated by the *splay* emphasis upon a widely diversified but ultimately symmetrical distribution of stubborn self-interest.

Another example of the *splay* type, as it falls away from the *splay* ideal, is found in the horoscope of Jay Gould.

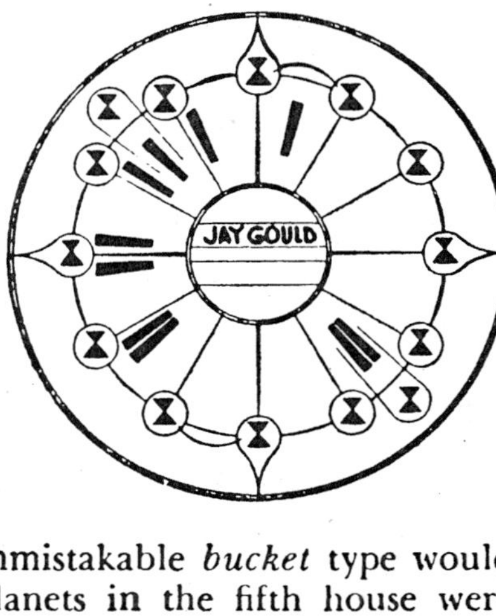

Here an unmistakable *bucket* type would be indicated if the two planets in the fifth house were in an exact conjunction, but the orb of eight degrees shows that they act separately for the most part in Gould's life, and this fact identifies the *splay* pattern's individualism. A *seesaw* classification might seem as legitimate as in the similar chart of Swedenborg, shown on page 93, but the two planets on the one side here suggest not so much the symmetry of the *seesaw* type as the raylike bunching which fundamentally characterizes the *splay* temperament. The *seesaw* pattern may have planets with a distinct tendency to bunch together, as illustrated in the horoscope of Oscar Wilde on page 99, but in his case the basic symmetry of the arrangement is dominant, while here the more distinctly irregular and raylike grouping is primarily evident.

Jay Gould is an outstanding prophet of rugged individualism. The broad ups and downs of this American financier ranged from constructive development of the country's transportation and industrial potentialities to the sheer chicanery by which he is best remembered, as in his attempt to corner gold with the resulting Black Friday panic of September 24, 1869. His capriciousness, his lack of concern over the interests of his fellows, and his capacity for turning from one emphasis to another as it suited him, are indicated by the partial bunching of his planets, which shows his real concentration of energies, and by the accompanying weakness of general integration in his planetary patterns, revealing the fatal diffusion of his efforts.

A further example of the *splay* type, as it falls away from the *splay* ideal, is found in the horoscope of Maximilien de Robespierre.

Here the *splay* pattern is seen in the purely freakish horoscope. The planets paired in the sixth and tenth houses in neither case are in a conjunction close enough to establish a *bucket* type. Moreover, a *bucket* classification would be prevented by the markedly irregular spacing of the planets in either of the possible bowl sections. By the same token, a close empty trine might make this a *locomotive* chart, but the classification is denied by the empty areas in the southeast and northwest quarters. The general symmetry might suggest a *seesaw* identification, but the bunching of the planets in two widely separated

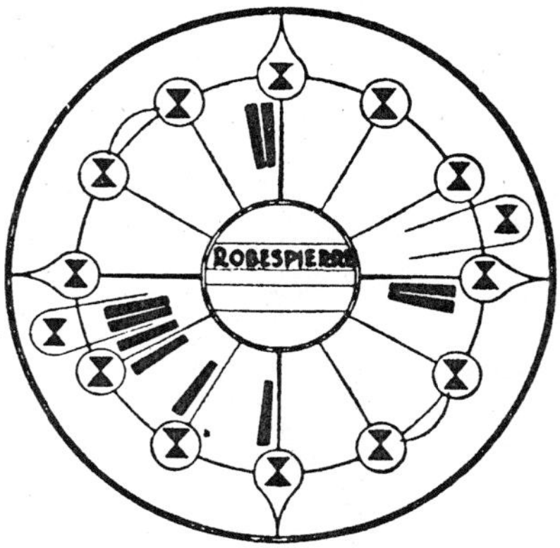

pairs on the southwest side, paralleling the case of Jay Gould in this raylike concentration, compels the *splay* typing.

Robespierre is the prophet of complete human ruthlessness. What could have been a great enduring contribution to human progress on his part was spoiled by his personal fearfulness, his psychological frustration. The perverse general symmetry of his highly individualized planetary grouping is a perfect portrait of his incomprehensible mixture of charm or abstract humanity on the one side, and an utter bestiality of spirit on the other. The horoscope does not call for the beast, necessarily, but it indicates a consummate power of undeviating fidelity to end-purposes, and this is highly accentuated by the coincident emphasis of the four angles. Few men in history have been as starkly foursquare in their course, for better or worse. The chart has a special value for the student through this emphasis, and a similar case in Appendix C is provided by Elbert Hubbard.

An example of the *splay* type as it approaches the ideal extreme, among contemporary or near-contemporary figures, is found in the horoscope of Carl Jung.

Here the chart is a *splash* potentiality with a distinct bunching at three points of definite rays, in two areas of concentration at the fourth and seventh angles. The tendency of the *splash* grouping to form bunches in this fashion has already been illustrated in the horoscope of Diamond-Jim Brady on page 25. Jung is classified as *splay* because his raylike emphases are functioning conjunctions, consisting of three aspects against none in Brady's case; that is, when the sun-Mercury-Venus combinations, which can never be disintegrated to any appreciable extent, are disregarded. Jung is the prophet of an important new "analytical psychology" which has escaped the excesses of the older faculty concepts, lifting man into a dynamic functional world where he may unscramble the various factors of his experience, and polish his skills through an intelligent examination and training of each in turn. Jung's prophetic insight is that man is an individual after all; that he may run up avenues of his choice, and specialize his experience along lines of his own choosing. The Swiss psychologist has taken the psychoanalytical technique out of its bondage to sex impulses, releasing man to be a creator rather than a creature of his circumstances.

The focal determination of the chart lies in the strong T cross in fixed signs, together with a preponderance of six planets in this quadrature. The point of stimulus in the T cross originally was the moon, and now is Pluto in addition. The emphasis on fixed signs endows Jung with his capacity to order ideas, to place the values of life in a structure of co-operative relations. The cross itself reveals

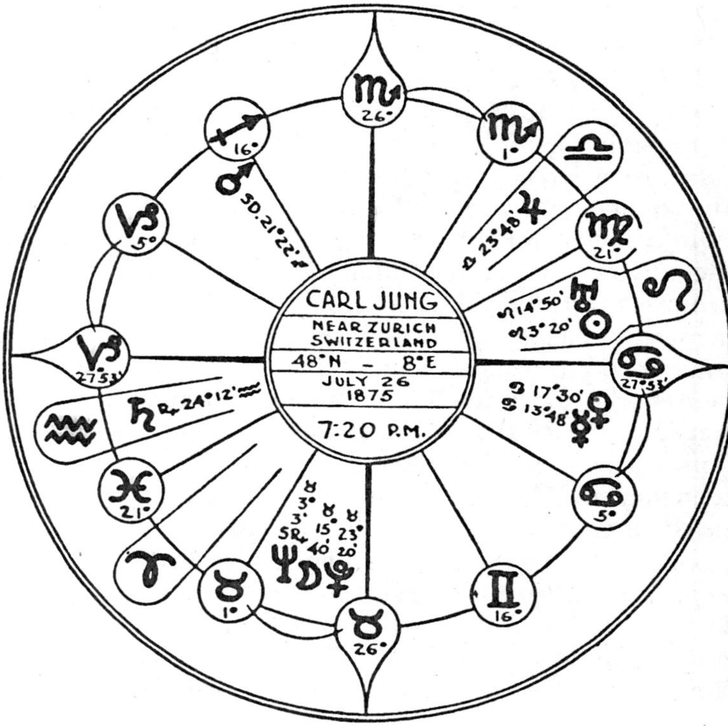

the dynamic in his tangible achievement. The moon pointing shows his capacity for reaching the public, or enlarging the racial understanding, while Pluto indicates his prophetic importance in directing this enlargement into the new channels of race-expression.

A second example of the *splay* type among contemporary or near-contemporary figures, and an illustration of deviation from the ideal extreme, is found in the horoscope of Algernon Swinburne.

Here the *splay* identification is suggested by the sheer individuality of the chart, in many respects similar to the horoscope of Robespierre. A *seesaw* classification is objectionable for the same reasons that prevail in the other's case, and a *bucket* typing would be denied by the raylike and tight clustering of the planets in the bowl section. Swinburne is the prophet of lyrical literature. He had the universality of the *splash* temperament, compressed uniquely into the single great gift of melody. His achievement is perhaps best seen in contrast with Robespierre, since he lifted the race to the same degree the Frenchman depressed it. Both acted in the name of beauty, and human freedom, under the width of their planetary spread, and both succumbed to the overrush of their own passions, a tendency indicated by the tightly bunched splay-points in these charts. The poet churned his life to produce a wonderful substance of rich poetry, whereas the lawyer kept his own life austere but turned the maelstrom of the French Revolution into far bloodier channels than it might otherwise have known. This dramatically illustrates the factor of free choice in life and experience.

The focal determination in Swinburne's chart is given by the T cross in fixed signs, accounting both for his capacity to sustain and direct his energies to his own ends, and for his primary interest in ideas and values. The point of stimulus is a retrograde Saturn in the creative sign of Scorpio, and in the house of self-expression. This reveals his introspective depth of understanding, as well as his extraordinary capacity to make it articulate. The stellium in Aries is an additional determinator, but only fully effective with the discovery of Pluto, long

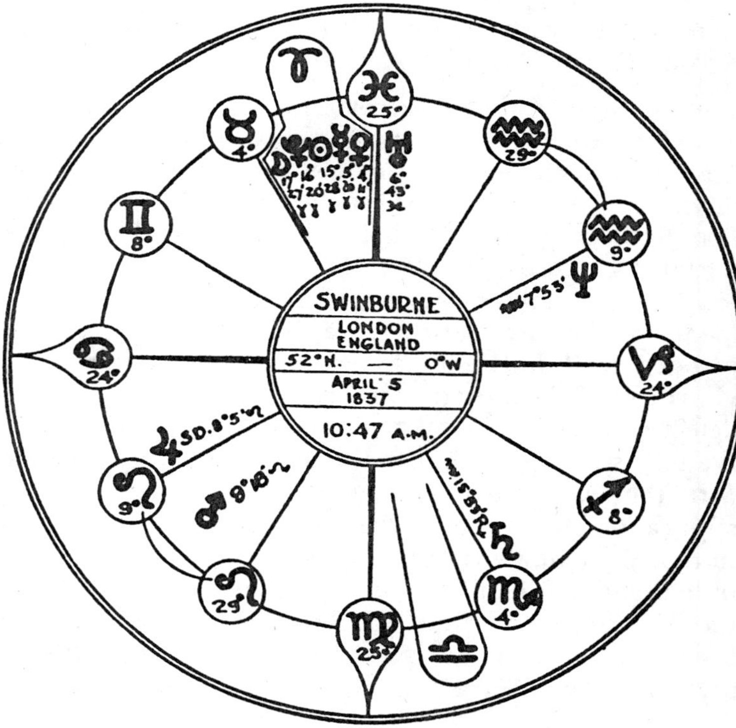

after the poet's death. This Aries emphasis shows his prophetic influence in its pioneer aspect, pertinent to the literary developments brought to a head with Pluto's discovery. The preponderance of seven planets in fire signs is a clue to the strength of Swinburne's inner nature or burning intuition, while the absence of any emphasis in earth signs discloses his need for a practical appreciation of the realities in everyday life.

A third example of the *splay* type among contemporary or near-contemporary figures, and an illustration of deviation from the ideal extreme, is found in the horoscope of Arthur Conan Doyle.

Here is a possible *bowl* pattern with the exaggerated concentration of planets found ideally in the *bundle* classification. The tendency of these two types to shade into each other has been illustrated in the charts of Edgar Allan Poe, on page 75, and William McKinley, on page 41. Sir Arthur's horoscope has the central clustering of planets found in McKinley's case, and also the rim emphasis which identifies the ideal *bowl* figure. The *splay* typing is demanded for him, however, because of the extreme individualism of the pattern. Sir Arthur is the prophet of the detective capacity in man. His Sherlock Holmes reveals the self-assurance of the *bowl* type, captured and blended with the *bundle* temperament's exceptional gift of self-application to an end of the moment, and the combination of the potentials is a striking illustration of the *splay* individual's efficient distribution of his energies in several special directions. Thus Sir Arthur's widely publicized interest in spiritism during the latter years of his life is a particular example of this diversified self-expression, but it is important not to confuse the *splay* type's specialized diversity with the *splash* type's simple spread of energy. The *splay* individual always has several major interests, but these remain characteristically separate.

The initial focal determination is provided by the T cross in fixed signs, linking Doyle with Jung and Swinburne in his critical talent, and equipping him with the same general dynamic type of idea-actuated enterprise. The point of stimulus is provided by Mercury in the twelfth house. This shows his basic mental temperament;

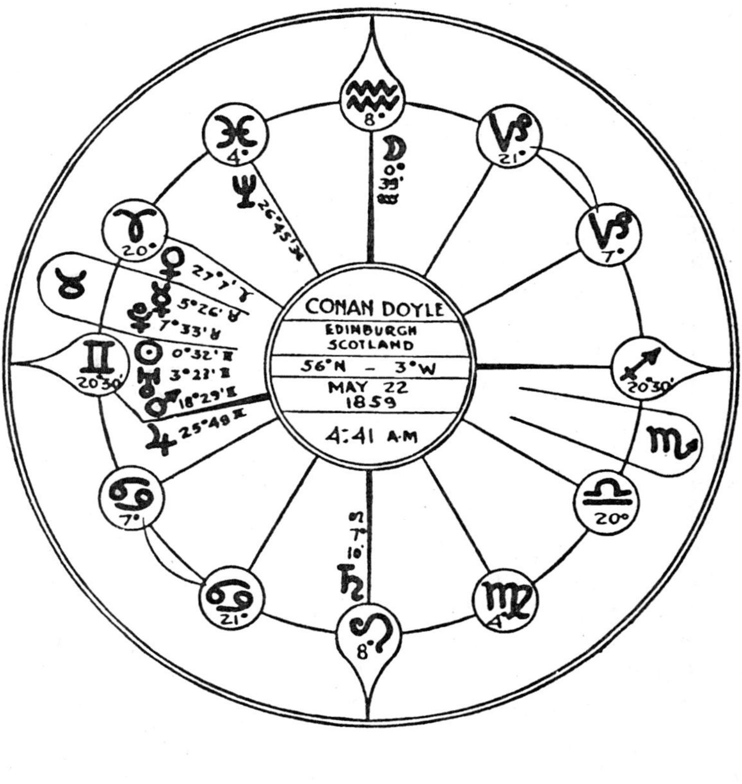

his concern over hidden things, whether in a Sherlock Holmes story or in the details of a séance. His stellium in Gemini greatly strengthens his power to vivify everything around him, and accounts for the genuine reality he gave to the celebrated fictional resident of Baker Street.

A fourth example of the *splay* type among contemporary or near-contemporary figures, and an illustration of deviation from the ideal extreme, is found in the horoscope of Andrew Carnegie.

Here the approach to the *locomotive* pattern on the one hand, and the *bucket* on the other, is a final illustration of the close linking of the *splay* temperament with each or all of the types, in one respect or another, even while it still reveals its own distinct temperament-set. The chart of Cecil Rhodes, given on page 51, is most like Carnegie's among the *locomotive* examples, and the horoscope of Lewis Carroll on page 87 is the nearest parallel to his patterning in the *bucket* illustrations. The three charts are exceptionally similar in the general spacing of the planets, but while the two planets which stand apart from the main clustering, in all three cases, are tied in with the other eight by a square or an opposition—that is, by a creatively integrating aspect—in the prior two horoscopes, in Carnegie's wheel they are wholly unrelated to the basic cluster in this essential respect, even though they are in square to each other. This is the fact which gives the most obvious clue to the necessity for a *splay* classification. Andrew Carnegie is the prophet of American commercial and industrial exploitation, and an excellent example of the man with many special and important interests. He not only performed a constructive service for the business world, but also set a pattern in philanthropy. He built a fortune for himself, and at the same time made all his associates rich. He has perpetuated his own ideals, and his inspiration to true individualism, through the string of Carnegie Libraries from one end of the country to another.

The focal determination in the chart is provided in part by the singleton Jupiter in the south, accepted as such since the exact degree on the ascendant is unknown. This

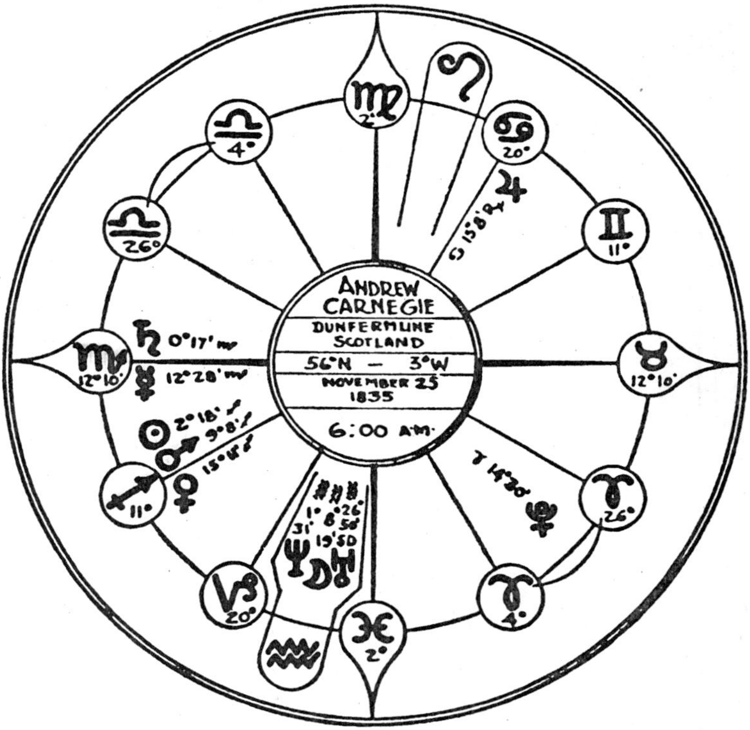

indicates that Carnegie's focus of all his activities is in a general expansion of himself, and everything around him, above the earth. There is also a lack of emphasis in the earth triplicity, and this accounts for his persistent efforts to achieve a real appreciation for life in all its practical phases, and to find ways for creating real opportunity for others as well as himself. The libraries give evidence of this inner driving urge to get some sense of human reality anchored in his day and age, while his determination to give away his money before he dies is not only a singleton Jupiter's generosity but a courageous effort to complement the lack of earth-sign emphasis.

HOW TO ORGANIZE THE PATTERN DETAILS

INTRODUCTION

THE METHOD OF PLANETARY PAIRS

AN ACCURATE astrological delineation not only requires that the horoscope be approached as a whole, and that any attempt to get at its meaning be guided by a preliminary disclosure of the general pattern, but also that the interpretation be ordered according to the whole at each stage of analysis. It is of little value to know that a man has a highly individualistic temperament under the *splay* type, and a dynamic concern with ideas through his focal determination in fixed signs, if his sun, intercepted in Leo, is said to give a frustrated egotism. The dramatic flair of Leo is always "ego" in a sense, and interception is "frustration" in an equally broad use of terms, but what might, in another pattern, indicate this inability of the native to gain acceptance of himself on his own terms, here simply reveals his protection from an undue external conditioning, and thus explains the creative self-sufficiency of his contribution to human knowledge. Reference in this example is to the horoscope of Carl Jung on page 111.

A young astrologer will often throw up his hands at the present point. "How am I ever going to learn to do that?" he will say.

The answer is, by a further employment of the same method of order which enables him to get at the whole-meaning of a chart through the seven types of temperament, and the outstanding focal determinators. The planets not only form patterns by the way in which they arrange themselves around the zodiac, and by the manner in which this arrangement is distributed through the house complex, but they have their distinctly individual activity. This has been considered only incidentally through the preceding chapters. The next step, in any guidance to horoscope interpretation, becomes the very necessary ordering of the planetary activities.

The most fundamental patterns of the horoscope are formed by the planets according to their place rather than their nature, by their aggregation or concentration rather than by any discrimination or analysis of their individual implications. This is a principle that cannot be emphasized too often. By the same token, however, it must never contribute to any neglect of the planets in the terms of their activity on their own account. Each has its characteristic contribution to make, by way of measuring a given individual's potentiality. Each also co-operates with the others in a composite life-at-work, and this is another and vital manifestation of patterning in the chart.

The ordering of the individual planetary activities is provided, not primarily by the positions of the ten bodies, but rather through the significance given their positions by certain fixed relationships among them. These are established on the basis of their nature, or fundamental identity. Certain planets have clearly defined functional ties with each other. Thus the sun has a natural connection with the moon, and in Carl Jung's chart the aspect between these two bodies gives him a nascent driving power which would utterly negate any notion of frustration. Instead it reveals struggle, continuing effort, critical determination.

The planetary activities fall into four departments, revealing four basic "lines of self-determination" in the horoscope. Each of these is a subpattern through which the planetary department provides a practical administration to the life-as-a-whole in some given and important direction. Here is the method of planetary pairs.

Section One

THE LINE OF VITALITY

The first planetary department consists of the sun and moon, which have been linked by astrologers since antiquity. As the "lights," these two planets give a primary indication of the life process.

The sun is the source or center of physical energy in the solar system. Astrologically it indicates the root of individual being in the most simple fact of existence *per se*, the fundamental urge of all life to continue to live. This is the "will" or purpose which not only is the basis of selfhood, but is the self's projection of itself into a determination to do things. It is the positive planet in the "department of life," and it reveals a given native's intention in every particular experience.

The moon is the mediator which reflects the light of the sun, giving a secondary distribution to the energies of the solar system and ruling the derivative relations in simple existence. It controls the tides of the ocean, as well as the organic rhythm of psychological forces in the living organism. Astrologically it indicates an individual's general experience with bodily necessities and group convenience. This is the "feeling" or response by which existence continues in association with other existence. The moon is the negative planet in the department. It reveals the native's conformity to his situation, his acquiescence in events.

The relation between the sun and moon, identifying

the most primitive act-of-selfhood in positive and negative phases, reveals the "line of vitality" in any chart, or the subpattern of simple existence. It charts a line because it shows with what type of activity the temperament will be vitalized most characteristically. The positions of the lights relative to each other is the clue to the manner in which the weight of the self will be directed instinctively in any issue. This self-stimulation in experience is the native's vitality.

The emphasis on this tie between the sun and moon, with the momentary subordination of every other aspect between either of these bodies and the eight remaining planets, establishes a pattern of order in the great complex of horoscopic relations. The remaining aspects are quite as important as the one between the lights, or between any of the particular pairs of planets which reveal the lines of self-determination in the four planetary departments, but they are not as useful for preliminary guidance in the horoscope's interpretation. Added to a recognition of the temperament-type, and an identification of the chart's focal emphasis, the four lines of fundamental self-expression become a sure basis of reference for the analysis of every activity in the life.

The aspects used for determining the basic patterns of a horoscope are the conjunction, sextile, square, trine and opposition. The parallel of declination has an equal antiquity, and is valuable in detailed work, but it has no part in the establishment of the zodiacal patterns because it is calculated from a different point of view. The minor aspects are effective when none of the five major ones are found, and in consequence are an important part of any full delineation of the chart, but they cannot be considered in defining the temperament-pattern because they indicate subordinate rather than primary relationships. An apparent exception to this is found in the quintile and septile, but these aspects, although unusual, are as primary as the square or trine. They have a special importance in focal determination, and must be taken into account whenever their orb is less than two whole degrees. In many cases a quintile or septile is also a sextile, since the sextile is an aspect which permits the full planetary orbs. In this text the quintiles and septiles are considered as they occur, under the head of either "sextile" or "no major aspect".

There are very few charts in which the sun and moon are not found in major aspect, since the sun takes an orb of seventeen degrees. In the other three departments, where ten-degree orbs are the largest permitted, better than half the cases will have no major relation between the two determining planets. The aspects are highly revealing when they are found, of course, but the lack of the major relationship between the members of a planetary pair is no less definitely significant. Moreover, any other accentuation of either planet making up the pair, or of both, whether in the focal determination or in the general house situation, is a supplementary factor of first importance in guiding the interpretation of a horoscope.

The Sun and Moon in a Conjunction Aspect

The meaning of the conjunction is always an emphasis of "activity" It is a concentration at one point of the various kinds of action represented by the planets involved. When the aspect is between members of a planetary department, that department becomes specially significant. In the present instance it shows an important stress upon the vitality, giving it unusual strength at the best and depriving it of all perspective at the worst.

Of the six cases of this aspect between the sun and moon, out of the twenty-eight horoscopes provided by the text in conventional form, none have either of the lights accentuated particularly in the temperament typing or focal determination, and only one reveals a special dignification by house position. This is the chart of Stephen Foster, on page 23, where the sun is the elevated planet. Whether Foster's focal determination be taken on the basis of the man in his own lifetime, with an emphasized midheaven axis and the stress placed on his interest in his artistic achievement rather than his practical welfare, or whether from the point of view of a prophetic influence surviving in his music, shown by the Pluto-pointed T cross in cardinal signs, the root of his vitality, under the conjunction of the sun and the moon, is a naïve willfulness or a basic temperamental ingenuousness. The sun's elevation indicates that he is always able to give importance to the circumstances of his life, or to muster a practical unthinking self-confidence by which he will feel that his inner resources are inexhaustible. The *splash* typing gives him a universal instinct, making each day adequate for itself. He has assurance, true or false, that there are always melodies ready to be composed, as his mood and need dictate.

An instance where the sun or moon may possibly have dignification by the house angles is provided by the horoscope of William James on page 35, but the houses are unknown. Neither the presence nor absence of such an indication can be assumed. It should be noted, however, that the moon cannot move out of the strong conjunction, no matter what the hour of birth may be. The special emphasis of vitality sharpens the self-contemplation of

James' *bundle* typing. It gives him that sense of a necessary self-sufficiency which, under Foster's *splash* temperament, leads to prodigality. James turns inward, to establish a combination of hypochondria and intense self-application in unusually original work. The conjunction of his lights conspires with the Capricorn stellium, and the singleton-in-disposition Saturn, to give him a lack of perspective on this fundamental level of experience which, rather than becoming improvidence, is a true single-mindedness.

The horoscope of William McKinley on page 41 is another case of the *bundle* type as emphasized by a line of vitality in naïve self-centeredness. This explains the ease with which he gave expression to his Aquarius stellium, rallying to the fight for the established American way of life when it was attacked by William Jennings Bryan. It also accounts for the lack of vital perspective with which, in a way now significant under the singleton Pluto above the earth, he furthered the political spoils system symbolized for his day by Senator Mark Hanna.

The chart of Cecil Rhodes on page 51 illustrates the basic vitality at its point of emphasis in a *locomotive* typing. Rhodes' focal determination, in a common-sign T cross, is aided by the underlying simplicity of his selfhood. The indication is given not only by the conjunction but by its position, in Cancer where things like Topsy "just grow", and in the seventh house where the sense of opportunism is developed. The two planets also are intercepted, which increases his basic or subjective naïveté. This inclines Rhodes, within the roots of himself, toward the very ingenuous although large scale humanitarian ideals through which his empire-building was accomplished.

The horoscope of Karl Marx on page 97 is an example of the simple emphasis of vitality in a frame of *seesaw* reaction to contrasts. His focal determination, the pairing tendency of his planets, is shown centered in a great ingenuousness of being by the exactness of this conjunction between his lights. The aspect not only indicates his complete lack of perspective in practical reality, but explains his success in creating a wholly new and theoretical structure for the world's economics, originally a panacea as much divorced from obligation to fact or conditioning by actuality as the man himself.

The chart of Algernon Swinburne on page 113 illustrates how a naïve foundation of self operates under the *splay* genius. The vitality emphasis lies in the Aries stellium, and Swinburne's underlying simplicity of self-determination finds expression in a pioneer gift of melody. He sings without inhibition, since Aries is intercepted and he is insulated from his fellows. The hard struggle of creative effort is undisturbed by any intruding perspective of self, under the conjunction of the lights. This is his great strength, but it is also the basis of his downfall because it gives him no instinctive warning against the onset of destructive self-indulgence.

The Sun and Moon in an Opposition Aspect

The meaning of the opposition is always "awareness" as an activity, or a sense of the alternative possibilities in act, and it is not so much an emphasis of experience at some particular point as it is a response to the usefulness of life and its resources. This indicates quite the reverse of a basic naïveté, and it reveals, in each of the four planetary departments, the native's more sophisticated or mature realization of his situation on the given level of experience. The practical evidence of this in the line of vitality is a dangerous vacillation in many cases, but also a valuable capacity to mobilize the best of the self's energies against each and every facet of a particular relationship.

Of four instances of this aspect among the example charts, three provide cases where the lights are strengthened by an accentuation in the general patterning. The horoscope of Luther Burbank on page 101 presents a moon which is very prominent, both as the point of application in his *seesaw* typing and as the elevated planet. Burbank was not only able to meet a public need in his achievement, through this pointing of his seesaw, and to win a worldwide recognition, which came to him almost completely unsought under the elevation of his moon, but he was exceptionally aware of the contrasting potentialities of all life at base. The patterning of his character produced resourcefulness rather than vacillation in the line of his vitality. He was able to mobilize himself in the light of problems that shifted continually in their call upon him, and this enabled the dynamic force of his fixed-sign cross to bear very real fruit in his career.

The chart of Henry Ford on page 49 shows the moon prominent as the leading planet in a *locomotive* typing, and it also participates in the fixed-sign T cross which becomes effective with Pluto's discovery. Ford, like Burbank, is drawn prominently before the public by this accentuation of the moon, coupled with his awareness of alternating potentialities under the influence of the opposition between the lights, but while the public relations were secondary with Burbank under his *seesaw* effort to balance his achievements in research, Ford literally compelled the world to make a path to his door under the *locomotive* type's persistence of impact upon the problems of the day. Moreover, Ford has the sun as a singleton in disposition, which explains the clear line of vitality in his basic self-desire, and reveals the opposition of the lights as resourceful self-mobilization rather than vacillation. The grand trine in air signs contributes to his basic versatility under the moon, and he thereby escapes any loss of himself in purposeless diffusion.

The horoscope of Oscar Wilde on page 99 has a rising sun, which stimulates the positive side of the awareness to potentialities shown by the opposition of the sun and moon. The aspect is within the widest allowable orb, but it is not very strong However, it explains the creative uncertainty and natural vacillation which led to Wilde's difficulties. His wavering in the roots of self makes him more than usually responsive to the grand trine in water. His strength is in his capacity, under his rising sun in connection with this water emphasis, for finding unlimited resources everywhere, and for the will to put them to use. This expresses the real power of the *seesaw* type. While he recognizes the antagonisms and contrasts in all life, he also sees that everything has its place in the universal solvent. He is only unable to get his own inner life centered in any genuine realization because he lacks the close tie to practical reality which brings the similar combination of a *seesaw* pattern and an opposition of the lights to a far different end in Burbank's case.

The chart of Evangeline Adams on page 85 shows no major accentuation of the sun and moon, to give special point to their opposition. Her keen awareness of the immediate potentials in any given situation, with the accompanying tendency to vacillation, is not made focal in any way in her experience, but it greatly increases the intensity of her interest in things, the single-minded quality of initiative she gains under her *bucket* typing. The minor prominence of the moon, through its opposition with her leading Mars, broadens the field of general opportunity into which her singleton-in-disposition Jupiter leads her.

The Sun and Moon Not in Any Major Aspect

The meaning of a lack of major aspect between the positive and negative planets in a department of planetary activity is that neither direct emphasis on action, nor individual awareness of potentialities, will characterize the native's experience on that particular level. Unless the two planets are prominent in some other fashion, the line of activity will be found subordinated to the focal pointing of the life in another direction. When this is the case in the department of life, the underlying vitality is adequate, that is, the vital economy remains a necessary part of existence, obviously, but is not a direct factor in the recurring decisions of day-by-day living.

Of the three instances, among the example horoscopes, in which no major aspect is found between the sun and moon, Diamond-Jim Brady's chart on page 25 presents the moon as an elevated planet, and exactly the same situation prevails in the charts of Abraham Lincoln on page 67, and William Jennings Bryan on page 83. This accentuation of the moon gives great prominence to the life, in some definite respect, but the touch with the public in these cases does not require any effort directed particularly to achieving that specific end, since the lights are not in aspect. The underlying vital relations of the life, in consequence, are never a conscious issue in experience.

Diamond-Jim Brady is the *splash* type's illustration of a man unconcerned over his own line of vitality. He is the very prophet of prodigality. The subordinated and unconditioned operation of his basic self-sustainment is an aid to him in his love for excitement, under the cardinal T cross, and also in preserving him from too great a sense of his own deficiency in articulating his deeper self-realization, under his lack of air-sign emphasis.

Abraham Lincoln illustrates this same free and unobtrusive line of vitality in the *bowl* type. His self-containment took form in his carelessness of health and his willing response to every public call, under the southern hemisphere-emphasis. There was never a time his physical organism was not adequate to carry him through the demands of a politician's cut-up routine.

William Jennings Bryan provides a demonstration by the *bucket* type of this same inner unconditioned freedom in the vital roots of self. The ease of physical self-sustainment, accompanied by the equal facility with which he gained social prominence under the elevated moon, aids the nozzlelike direction of energies under this pattern, and encourages the Sir Lancelot rôle which he preempted for himself under his singleton Mars.

The Sun and Moon in a Square Aspect

The square is the first of the aspects which distribute experience in the patterns of group action, or make activity a matter of joint act with people or situations. What is indicated, therefore, is in sharp contrast with the conjunction, opposition and lack of major aspect, or the cases where action is more wholly a matter of the self and its subjective relations. The meaning of a square is always a "construction" activity. It identifies a situation at some critical point, involving struggle for those who participate in the given relationship, and strain for whatever is especially concerned. The primary matter at issue is never the nature or condition of the native's life, but rather the state of affairs in something he is attempting to accomplish. The stress lies in the problems of adjustment or re-adjustment of self to factors which lie entirely outside self.

Of four instances of this aspect in the line of vitality among the example charts, that of Leon Trotsky on page 21 has the moon emphasized as the point of stimulus in a fixed-sign cross, and this one of the lights is also the rising planet. In consequence, no matter what Trotsky does under the indication of his horoscopic pattern, it must be public in nature, and must have significance for his fellows. Because his lights are in square aspect, any interpretation of his chart must be guided not only by its *splash* typing, which endows him with his universal interest, and by its emphasis of fixed signs, which gives him his concern with the utopian ideals of Communism, but also by the realization that it is a necessity of his organism, if he is to live, to engage in struggle as a means of existence; to participate in the hard labor of building something as a fundamental exercise of selfhood.

The horoscope of Carmen Sylva on page 37 has no emphasis of the lights through the *bundle* typing, nor through the focal determination, but it may have the rising moon found in Trotsky's chart, and an elevated sun in addition. The prominent placing of these planets by house greatly strengthens the influence of Carmen Sylva's department of life, and shows that she is largely successful through her sheer vitality. The unusual concentration of her interests, shown by the tight *bundle* pattern, together with the enhancement of her creative gifts, through the Capricorn stellium with its Saturn as a singleton in disposition, is supplemented by the square of the sun and moon. The demand for struggle, for a definite effort at building things, prevents her from slipping off or losing herself in the depths of her own being, and makes her experience more significant than it would be otherwise.

In the charts of Upton Sinclair on page 53, and Carl Jung on page 111, the moon has special emphasis as the point of stimulus in a T cross. The indication is stronger in Jung's horoscope because the cosmic cross is a definite fixed-sign configuration, whereas in Sinclair's case a common-sign opposition is built into the T cross by the moon in a cardinal sign. The importance of the lesser light in both lives accounts for their public careers, and the square aspect particularly strengthens the capacity of both for hard and sustained effort in their creative work. The *locomotive* typing gives Sinclair, of the two men, a greater persistence of impact on the social problems which have become his life interest, quite irrespective of results. In consequence, his grand trine in earth signs is brought to a point of constructive contribution greater than might normally be expected, and the configuration's tendency to diffusion becomes an asset in a gift for wide orientation. Jung's *splay* typing, by contrast, together with his lack of the grand trine, eliminates any danger that he will waste his energies, but presents instead the real problem of an adequate outlet for the mental energy indicated by his unusual fixed-sign emphasis. The square of the lights in his case compels a constructive employment of the flashing intuitions that pour in upon him.

The Sun and Moon in a Trine Aspect

The meaning of the trine is always "creation", or a flowing activity. This generally takes the form of a broad momentum, and the ease of its course has made the trine the most desired of all planetary relations in an older or more superficial astrology. When the line of vitality has a momentum through this aspect, provided only it is the sort the native desires, the life is very rich; he knows a very genuine satisfaction.

Of the five cases of this aspect between the lights, the horoscope of Helen Keller on page 69 shows the moon emphasized as the leading planet in a *bowl* typing. The free flow of her vitality, enhanced by the unusual public co-operation gained through this leading moon in the *bowl* temperament, greatly strengthens the chances for her remarkable achievement. Her western hemisphere-emphasis takes on the function of opportunity instead of bondage, since the line of vitality emphasizes momentum rather than struggle. She is guided by events, rather than thwarted.

The charts of Theodore Roosevelt on page 19, and Sir Arthur Conan Doyle on page 115, illustrate the free flow of the fundamental line of vitality as this is accentuated by one or the other of the lights as an elevated planet. The sun in Roosevelt's case makes his conscious will dominant in his life, and gives him a sense of purpose and motive with his backing of easy momentums in his underlying vitality. His smooth basic self-integration supplements the functioning of his T cross configurations, and furthers the exhibition of immediate personality-actuated and ultimate idea-inspired projects through his basic *splash* typing.

The moon is Sir Arthur's elevated planet, and this contributes more to the passive popularity under which a *splay* temperament best expresses its highly individual interests. The Englishman, with his T cross in fixed signs, has the capacity for manipulating ideas which characterizes the American in his surviving influence, but his touch with personality through a common-sign emphasis is given by the stellium in Gemini rather than by a cosmic cross, a contrast which shows how his smooth flowing vitality is directed into channels of creative workmanship, rather than into administrative leadership.

The trine between the lights in the horoscopes of Jeff Davis on page 39, and George Gershwin on page 57, is not supplemented by any other emphasis of either planet in the focal determination or house complex. As a result the simple momentum of the line of vitality in these instances is merely an unconditional endowment of the life on this first or primary level of experience. Jeff Davis technically has a moon singleton above the earth, but better guidance in the interpretation of his chart is gained by noting, primarily, the co-operation of the lights with the general tendency of his planets to form pairs. The pairing reveals a determination to be significant, and the free flow of his fundamental vitality equips him with a valuable insouciance, or a capacity for a complete and thoroughgoing self-dramatization.

The same simple revelation of basic selfhood is expressed through the channels of his art by George Gershwin. With a grand trine in air signs, and a T cross in common signs, he is under great necessity for making a continual use of his intellectual spread under the one, and his general interest in human relations under the other. His capacity for an effective impact on problems and issues under the *locomotive* typing adds to his need for worlds to conquer. The line of vitality gives him an easy momentum in any enterprise to which he might care to turn a hand, enabling him to use his physical energy to the fullest extent.

The Sun and Moon in a Sextile Aspect

The meaning of the sextile is always an activity of a co-operative, assistance or "production" order. In many respects the aspect acts as a minor trine. Therefore, when the key planets of any of the four departments are in sextile to each other, the particular line of self-determination is brought to its point of most practical or everyday manifestation. This is usually pleasing to the native, since it involves even less of a demand upon him than the trine.

Of the six instances of a sextile between the sun and moon, the one in the horoscope of Edgar Allan Poe on page 75 is somewhat questionable because the hour of birth is not known. Neither of the lights, barring the possibility of rising or setting positions, is emphasized in any way. The chart is the *bowl* type, with a consequent self-containment, and the expansive Jupiter is a singleton in disposition in the Pisces stellium, giving an accentuated poetic appreciation and a capacity for an unusually genuine soul-expression. As a result the line of vitality fills a conveniently subordinate or co-operative rôle. Poe's energies are wholly his, to use as he wills, even when he chooses to plunge himself into the most destructive self-indulgence.

This subordination of the line of vitality in the general pattern of a life is characteristic in similar fashion of the charts of Abdul Baha on page 73, and of Andrew Carnegie on page 117. Any constructive guidance to the interpretation, at this point, is merely the observation that their economy of energies will always be normal, and never a matter of particular issue in experience. In neither case is either light emphasized by the focal determination or house complexion.

The horoscope of Lewis Carroll on page 87 shows the moon specially emphasized as the rising planet, and also as leading planet in the bowl segment. As a result the momentum of his life acquires a public appeal, which is of great aid to him in expressing his rather delicate genius. No struggle of surging energies within him impedes his effort to complement, in this fashion, the absence of water-sign emphasis in his pattern. He cultures a creative intensity under his *bucket* temperament, but it is quiet, both under Saturn as a handle planet, and under the still momentum of a sun and moon in sextile.

The two remaining examples of sextile aspect between the lights are more properly cases of quintile, which always indicates a special talent or "artistry". The horoscope of Paul von Hindenburg on page 103 illustrates the quintile's activity in his development of a line of vitality into a true art of efficiency, supplementing his genius for rising to an emergency under the cardinal emphasis, and making him the hero of the German people. This quintile of his sun and moon expands his capacity for seeing all the possibilities of a given situation, under the *seesaw* typing, into an unusually powerful and positive momentum, quite different from the mere drift of a sextile.

The Hindenburg horoscope is an extreme borderline case in the determination of aspects, since the lights are exactly at the midpoint between their sextile and their square positions, and therefore may be taken in either relationship, as well as quintile. This is due to the unusually wide orb allowed for the sun. In all other instances, when neither the sun nor the moon is involved, the orb of the quintile begins where the orb of the sextile ends, and does not reach to the orb of the square at all; so that the threefold possibility never has to be faced. Here, where the lights stand at the midpoint of the potential between the two major aspects, they actually express the real genius of the quintile, although this operates with a three-degree orb, such as is never properly allowed otherwise for either the quintile or septile. These considerations are the fine points of judgment that come with practice, and that are grounded in a broad general understanding—a basic common sense—rather than in any encyclopedic knowledge of rules or aphorisms.

The chart of George Bernard Shaw on page 89 has an exceptionally exact quintile of the lights. This gives more than the sextile's co-operation with a *bucket* typing, which of all the seven temperament groups has a distinct flair for talent, an individualized genius in self-expression. Shaw's egoistic artistry, as a basic energy-expenditure, has prevented him from wasting any opportunity to interpret the foibles of the world to itself, his pioneer work under a west-singleton Mars. His sun as a singleton in disposition brings everything in his life to its special pointing in the terms of his own will to be what he wants to be, and under the influence of the sun's quintile he can develop a prophetic self-realization which at times may soar to very great heights.

Section Two

THE LINE OF PERSONALITY

THE second planetary department consists of Jupiter and Saturn, the two bodies, out of the seven known to the ancients, which were observed to lie particularly apart from the earth and the sun, or to make their circuits toward the outer boundaries of the energy-system. Their influence seemed to be directed toward whatever was remote or indirect in man himself, that is, his inner or spiritual being, and in consequence they were linked in a "department of soul".

Jupiter is the larger, brighter and nearer of these two greater planets in the ancient system, and in astrology it represents the expansive nature of things, or direct experience with the illimitable inner resources of self. Here is the self's "enthusiasm", or the objective side of the soul in the form of consciousness. Jupiter measures the individual's willingness to enter into experience, or to expend the real substance of his own being. It is the positive planet in the department, revealing the degree of whole-souledness with which any native participates in events.

Saturn is the smaller, less distinct and more distant of the original greater planets, and in astrology it represents the contracting and compressing nature of things, or the experience gained in any retreat from the outer fact of life. This is the subjective or mental side of the soul, man's "sensitiveness" as it takes the form of understanding and wisdom on the best side, fear and suspicion on the worst. It indicates the capacity of the soul to withdraw from experience, or to return into the depths of itself when the resources of being are inadequate to meet some situation. It is the negative planet in the department, and it reveals the native's basic reactions to remote or deep stimulus.

The relation between Jupiter and Saturn, measuring the self-conscious side of self in positive and negative phases of valuation and desire, reveals the "line of personality" in any chart. Here is the subpattern of personal existence, in contrast with the simple and fundamental vitality indicated by the sun and moon relationship. Personality is selfhood on a conscious level of life. Jupiter and Saturn show the conditions under which the native is able to manipulate the consequences of experience, whether in terms of character or of life situation. They chart the living relations by which man gains an individual certification of his being, an assurance that his efforts have some enduring worth.

Jupiter and Saturn in a Conjunction Aspect

The horoscope of William James is the only illustration of this aspect among the twenty-eight examples. The fundamental direction of his life is through the highly centered emphasis of his physical energies, as has been brought out by the analysis on page 125 f. The line of personality intensifies this emphasis, making it exceptionally focal on the conscious side of his experience. He not only has the conjunction of Jupiter and Saturn, but his Saturn, as a singleton in disposition, is the most important planet in his chart. The unusual emphasis of the department's negative planet also means that his interest centers more in the end-results and consequences of his work than in any pleasure he might have had in the immediate performance. The subpattern of soul thus accounts for his development as a philosopher of major importance.

Jupiter and Saturn in an Opposition Aspect

The twenty-eight examples provide no illustrations for this type of personality pointing. When it is found it indicates that the native will have a constant and conscious awareness of his personal place in the scheme of things, and this is shown in the case of George Washington, the full details of whose horoscope are given in Appendix C. Jupiter, in addition, is the leading planet in Washington's *locomotive* patterning, which explains the degree to which he courted responsibility, deliberately laying the foundations for his place as the father of his country.

Jupiter and Saturn Not in Any Major Aspect

There are seventeen cases, among the example charts, where the line of personality is made subordinate to others of the four lines, in a greater or less degree, by the lack of a major aspect between the planets in this department of soul. The horoscope of Lewis Carroll is important because Saturn has an exceptional emphasis, despite the failure of Jupiter to complete an opposition. Saturn is not only a singleton in two different hemispheres, but is also the handle in a *bucket* typing, and is the elevated planet. Saturn accentuates Carroll's distinctly inner sensitiveness to the course of life around him, already pointed out on page 137. It sharpens the critical functioning of his personality, even though the absence of a direct relation with Jupiter denies him that conscious sense of personality and its powers which is exhibited in George Washington's case.

In the chart of Carmen Sylva, where the life is almost completely centered through the vitality pattern analyzed on page 132, Saturn is a singleton in disposition. This gives the Rumanian queen a distinct gift of sensitiveness, a refined ordering of her experience through her depth of consciousness. Like Lewis Carroll, she lacks the self-assertiveness of a functioning line of personality, but she also, like him, has an exceptional but quiet acumen. The emphasis in her life is completely self-centered, since these first two lines of self-determination are the only ones effective in her horoscope. She was at no point as much the queen as the authoress. Because of this limited emphasis in her planetary departments, no further analysis of the subpatterns is required for an effective guidance in the interpretation of her chart.

The horoscope of Leon Trotsky, although devoid of personality emphasis otherwise, has an elevated Saturn. This sharpens his experience or capacity to learn lessons in public affairs. It gives him a very important decisiveness, when it comes to meeting crises. He is able to face any question of choice, along the lines of his particular interests as these have been indicated on page 132, in a very impersonal way.

In five cases, out of the seventeen where the line of personality is at no time the basis of any real crisis in the life, and where Saturn has no emphasis in the basic patterning, Jupiter brings the department of soul to a point of special importance through a definite intensification of the native's spontaneity, his gift for a free and full participation in experience. In the horoscope of Edgar Allan Poe, this planet is a singleton in disposition. The resulting general pattern of activity in his temperamental make-up, already outlined on page 136, is given a personal direction through his art, or through his definitely conscious capacity to put the whole of himself into whatever he does. The lack of an integrating aspect in his line of personality results in a tendency to develop an enthusiasm rather than a discrimination of conscious self-expression.

Andrew Carnegie's chart presents Jupiter as a singleton above the earth. The outward expansiveness of his personality, indicated by this position of the department's positive planet, adds little basic integration to Carnegie's life since the simple free flow of vital energy, described on page 136, has offered no fundamental need of self-realization, and since there is no aspect here to give a real bottom to the Scottish steel-master's experience. Jupiter strengthens the activity of a *splay* patterning, but the result is close to a mere capriciousness on these two levels of self-centering.

The horoscope of Cecil Rhodes is a case somewhat similar to Carnegie's, but the emphasis of Jupiter in the Rhodes chart is as the leading planet in a *locomotive* typing, which gives a positive willingness to accept responsibility, and in many respects supplements the lack of a Jupiter-Saturn aspect. However, while some element of self-sensitiveness in the general opportunism is provided by the Jupiter emphasis, there is no genuinely conscious self-integration, and the basic ingenuousness of the life, indicated on page 126, is increased on this level, rather than brought into check.

The chart of Paul von Hindenburg gains a very definite focus in spontaneous personality by the position of Jupiter as the point of emphasis in his cardinal T cross, but there is no integration of his self-centered activities on the conscious level, and as a result his exceptional facility for doing things or getting them done, pointed out in the analysis on page 137, reveals him in certain curious respects as almost an automaton, a man practically devoid of any true interior life.

The horoscope of Arthur Conan Doyle has its emphasis in the department of soul through a rising Jupiter. This adds a spontaneity of self-expenditure to the general and easy momentum of his life, analyzed in its distinctly passive aspect on page 134 f., but does not give any conscious integration of the personality. The prominence of Jupiter here accentuates the *splay* type of distinct individualism, given a public significance by an elevated moon, but Sir Arthur is in no wise challenged to know himself inwardly, or to take any definite control of the drift in his affairs.

In addition to these eight cases of particular pointing in the life through the special emphasis of Saturn or Jupiter, each acting independently of the other, there is one instance in which the two planets, devoid of major aspect between them, are yet strongly linked through a quintile. This is in the chart of Stephen Foster. It indicates the genuinely personal artistry which becomes a conscious foundation for the composer's creative gifts. It brings soul, in the form of sweetness and purity, into his melodies, and gives him an integration through his art which he lacks in any ordinary or normal sense, thus compensating him for the temperamental irresponsibility which was disclosed by the analysis on page 125.

In the eight remaining instances where there is no major aspect between Saturn and Jupiter, and no supplementary emphasis of either of them, out of the twenty-eight examples, the general subordination of the department of soul simply indicates the general ingenuousness of a personality seldom brought to a point of issue. These people feel under no necessity whatever, at any time, to make any accounting to themselves for the state or progress of their own works. The most clean-cut of these examples is provided by William McKinley, and the extent to which the whole focus of his self-centered side of existence is thoroughly naïve has been definitely intimated on page 126.

In three cases the relatively complete ineffectiveness of the line of personality has had an important compensation in the correspondingly more than usual emphasis of a focus in self-activity, through the level of experience established by the line of vitality. Reference here is to the horoscopes of Henry Ford, Oscar Wilde and Luther Burbank, to which a careful consideration is given on pages 128-9.

In two other cases the unconditioned freedom or innocence of the native in his line of personality has acted as a definite encouragement to an easy drifting under a trine aspect in the line of vitality. This is similar to the situation in Conan Doyle's chart, but without the rising Jupiter which strengthens Doyle's department of soul. The extreme instance of the combination will give the native an exceptional capacity for throwing himself into the convenience of any given state of affairs. This may be a complete lack of discrimination, at the worst, but an exceptionally unified self-centering at the best. The charts of Jeff Davis and Helen Keller illustrate the benefits derived from the fullness of momentum here. The lack of inhibition which characterized the king of the hobos has been described on page 135. The value of the blind woman's unrestrained and undirected self-mobilization, becoming opportunity within the bounds of her limitation, is explained on page 134.

The horoscope of William Jennings Byran provides another instance of unconditioned self-expenditure, but under a radically different emphasis. He is the first of two examples where there is no major aspect between the key planets on either level of self-centered experience. His basic naïveté has been described on page 130 f., and the totally unaccentuated line of personality here reveals the danger that he may plunge into everyday experience without the least discrimination.

Bryan has important compensation in the two remaining departments, but the chart of Abraham Lincoln is exceptional among the twenty-eight examples, since it is the only one in which there is no major aspect between the members of the key pairs in any one of the planetary lines of determination. Lincoln is revealed as a distinctly out-of-time or cosmic figure. Any detailed analysis of his life must be guided by a continual emphasis on this one salient factor of complete unconditioned simplicity. Lincoln, taken astrologically, is almost the incarnation of a higher principle of human idealization, rather than a normal man of appetites and ambitions. His transcendence of physical limitations, described on page 130 f., is now supplemented by an insight into his utter naturalness at the core of his own personality. His frustration was not so much in failing to gain his desires as in his inability to integrate himself in a way that would fit the superficial inanities of a world in which he was alien.

Jupiter and Saturn in a Square Aspect

All four cases of this aspect, among the example horoscopes, supplement the necessity for struggle in the line of personality, or for a consciously creative work on the native's part, with other very strong indications in this department of soul. Evangeline Adams, whose keen awareness of the potentials of outer life has been summarized on page 129 f., is greatly endowed in real personality, not only by her Jupiter as a singleton in disposition, but by her elevated Saturn. The complete dominance of the other planets by Jupiter reveals her capacity for a personal concern with things, as well as her willingness to accept responsibility, while her ninth-house Saturn emphasizes the sense of proportion that prevails in her life at all times, giving her the practical discrimination responsible for her success.

Jupiter is accentuated in the horoscope of Diamond-Jim Brady as the point of stimulus in his all-important cardinal T cross. This intensifies his struggle on the level of conscious self-realization, and leads to his continual desire to find himself in a deeper sense by helping others. He is largely inarticulate in sharing his more worthwhile experience, however, because Jupiter is retrograde and intercepted. His response to the challenge in his line of personality enables him to derive considerable enduring benefit from the superficial prodigality described on page 130 f.

The naïve self-centering found in the chart of Algernon Swinburne, and analyzed on page 127, provides a somewhat similar situation. The Saturn focus in his T cross makes it necessary for him to search for deeper values in the ideas with which he works, and the necessity for struggle in his line of personality forces him to carry the agonizing of his soul-activity out into life, where it can become the basis of his poetry.

George Bernard Shaw is saved from taking his own high talents too lightly by this necessity for conscious struggle within himself, under the square aspect in his department of soul. The unusual nature of his basic life-emphasis has been pointed out on page 137 f., and this is given an extra personal stress by his rising Saturn. He is kept more sensitive to his whole real-self, or the resources of being shown by the second house, than his singleton-in-disposition sun might ever permit him to admit. The sun by its nadir position throws all outer emphasis in his life to the line of personality, and his fertile ego is brought to operate, not by self-assertion, but by the agonizing creation of a genuine personage.

Jupiter and Saturn in a Trine Aspect

The only case of a full natural momentum in the line of personality, among the twenty-eight examples, is found in the horoscope of Carl Jung. The supplementary influence of a rising Saturn, paralleling Shaw's situation, equips Jung with a valuable personal sensitiveness, and enhances his conscious realization of opportunities for employing his surplus mental energies, revealed by the analysis of his case on page 133. The ease of function on this level of personal relations has provided the real basis for his career as a psychologist, since it gives him an easy access to the case histories he needs.

Jupiter and Saturn in a Sextile Aspect

Of the five examples of a sextile aspect in the department of soul, three have special interest because the two planets are also in a close septile. The meaning of a septile aspect is that the native's life, in respect to the common activity ruled by the planets which form it, is not so much characterized by the simple and over-facilitated drift of the sextile, or by the specially refined and talented free flow of the quintile, as by a strange and inexorable momentum or "fatality" of action which must take place, instinctively or consciously, in response to an apparent inevitability in circumstances.

The horoscope of Theodore Roosevelt affords a simple illustration of the septile's operation in the roots of conscious personality. Roosevelt seemed to feel the whip-lash of a deep driving necessity throughout his life, and he expressed this in his strenuous philosophy. His extraordinarily broad, will-directed and basic momentum, summarized in its vitality aspect on page 134, can be seen in its deeper origin as a manifestation of this septile. The place of Saturn as the point of stimulus in his T cross in fixed signs reveals the personal sensitiveness by which every idea, in the surviving influence of his career, has a definite value to the race under the new developments coming into being with Pluto.

Abdul Baha's chart is an example of particular value because a complete guidance to its interpretation, as was the case with Carmen Sylva, is provided on the two levels of self-centered experience. The free and quite non-distinctive flow of Abdul Baha's line of vitality has been pointed out on page 136, and the relative ease of conscious expression, indicated here by the fundamental sextile, is merely an additional clue to a life characterized by too much fluidity of function in its basic make-up. The situation is saved by the rising position of Jupiter, making it necessary for him to put himself whole-souledly into whatever he does, and by the position of Saturn as the point of application in his bowl, making it impossible for him to accomplish anything without high personal sensitiveness to some definite mission in life. This focal association of the key planets in the department of soul is intensified by their nearly exact septile, and a consequent truly extraordinary strengthening of his line of personality. The lack of all further self-determination is a testimony to personal nature of his prophetic rôle.

The horoscope of George Gershwin provides the third case of septile aspect in this department, and the great compulsion in his soul's creative activity is the fluid flow of his over-abundant vitality as this reveals itself in the line of personality. The position of Saturn as a rising planet intensifies the practical impact of the septile on his career, making him as sensitive as Shaw and Jung to the opportunities of his situation. It discourages any needless waste of the psychological energies described in the analysis on page 135.

The horoscope of Karl Marx, viewed in the light of its preliminary pointing on page 127, shows the simple co-operation of the line of personality under the sextile, and this is little more than a confirmation of the native's basic ingenuousness. The central focus of his life on a conscious level is revealed by the position of Saturn as an elevated planet, which gives him an all-essential sensitiveness to the world situation, and which results also in giving a practical turn to utopian efforts which otherwise might have lost themselves in fantasy.

The career of Upton Sinclair has been given its direction to a large extent by the position of Jupiter as a leading planet in his *locomotive* typing. This has contributed to the smooth momentum of a line of personality under the sextile, and it reveals his important willingness to accept responsibility. In general his conscious sense of self remains subordinate to his perception of the task to be done, and supplements the significance of the analysis given his chart on page 133.

Section Three

THE LINE OF EFFICIENCY

The first two planetary departments have comprised the self-centered side of the native's existence. His vitality is what he is, in and of himself, and his personality reveals the fundamental adjustments he must make within himself, continually, in his relations with the world around him. Experience in general, however, has its less subjective side also, in the group-centered type of activity where everything is known externally, or through convenience, nearness, availability, usefulness and the like. An individual breathes of necessity, but he puts down one object and picks up another only as they take on meaning or value. The group-centered realm embraces acquired relations, or definite objects as they acquire actual significance in experience.

The third planetary department consists of Mars and Venus, with Mercury as an additional member. It has been observed from antiquity that these planets are important through their adjacency to other bodies. Mars and Venus have orbits next to the earth. Mercury is next to the sun. They are neither primary bodies, like the lights, nor remote ones with a relatively symbolical significance, like Jupiter and Saturn. In consequence these planets have been taken as the basic indicators of things; that is, of objects into which meaning or value is placed, in which the pertinency is loaned or results from the accident of place and position. Here is the "department of affairs".

Mercury has no true adjacency to the earth, but accompanies the sun, which in turn takes on the earth's movement in the zodiac. This gives Mercury a secondhand or substitute relation to the earth, and it becomes the ruler of "mind," or the faculty for substitute, abstract, secondhand, and vicarious experience. This is a mediated or intellectual relationship with the affairs at hand. Mercury is thus of exceptional importance in the detailed delineation of a chart, but it has no part in identifying the native's lines of self-determination.

Mars is the outermost planet, of the two with orbits next to the earth, and it represents the outreach of man, or shows how an individual starts things. It is easy to confuse the meaning of Mars and Jupiter, but there will be no difficulty if Mars is recognized as "initiative" or the practical, everyday and purely objective act-of-being in the direct use of things. It measures man's simple manipulation of the world, rather than self, and shows his exterior rather than interior attack on the problems of life. Mars is the positive planet in the department, and it reveals the immediate application of the native's efforts in any given situation.

Venus, as the innermost planet of these two, indicates the acquisitive capacity of man in a very literal or objective sense, or shows how he finishes things. This is the native's "appreciation", or his more or less conditioned and ordinary routine activity in the conservation and refinement of things on the one hand, and in the consumption, condemnation and destruction of them on the other. It is the negative planet in the department, identifying the ulterior and aesthetic application of an individual's energies to the immediate problems of the group economy.

The relation between Mars and Venus, measuring the group-centered experience of self in positive and negative phases of the practical and objective business of existence, reveals the "line of efficiency" in any chart. Here is the subpattern through which an individual maintains himself in an everyday world, or becomes effective among his fellows. Mars and Venus show the native's capacity to handle the various practical enterprises to which he may turn a hand in a human society. This includes affairs of the heart as well as the head, and of the intellect or mentality as well as the hands or physical skill.

Mars and Venus in a Conjunction Aspect

The horoscopes of Andrew Carnegie and Lewis Carroll are the only illustrations of this aspect among the twenty-eight examples. Mercury is the rising planet in Carnegie's case, revealing an important emphasis in his line of efficiency even though Mercury is a supernumerary planet in the departmental subpattern. The conjunction gives both Carnegie and Carroll a high concentration of interest in detailed affairs, and it also betrays their deficiency in practical or everyday perspective. The compensation in Carnegie's chart, through the rising Mercury, shows that he has an unusually keen mental insight, or a native canniness, which provides a measure of practical direction to the general broad expansiveness, analyzed in terms of its dangerous lack of integration, on page 143.

The line of efficiency is not strengthened in other directions for Lewis Carroll. In consequence his everyday activities are somewhat limited, and his life is left centered in the particular sensitiveness explained on page 141. The limited relationship of both Carnegie and Carroll to group experience is not only indicated by this narrowed focus in the subpattern of affairs, but the fourth of the planetary departments has no added contribution to make to their lines of self-determination, and as a result the preliminary analysis of their horoscopes is complete at this point.

Mars and Venus in an Opposition Aspect

No illustrations of this type of focus, showing the individual with a hyperacute sense of the real or illusory potentialities in his immediate circumstances, is provided by any of the charts presented in the main text, but an example will be found in the horoscope of Joseph Stalin, cited in connection with the Trotsky analysis on page 21. Stalin's characteristically basic reaction to external factors, rather than to internal conviction, is indicated by the unusual exactness and emphasis of this aspect in his case, coupled with his lack of major aspect between Jupiter and Saturn.

Mars and Venus Not in Any Major Aspect

The most important examples, among the sixteen cases where the line of efficiency becomes subordinate to other lines of emphasis among the subpatterns, are found in the charts of William Jennings Bryan and Abraham Lincoln, since both these men are marked also by an unusual lack of self-centered integration in their lives. Bryan's all-important compensation is provided first in the department of affairs, by his west-singleton Mars strengthened because this planet is also the handle in his *bucket* patterning. His unconditioned self-expenditure, analyzed on page 146, is held to the service of every situation in which he finds himself, because of the west singleton, and the fact that this planet is Mars inclines him to play the pioneer. His affairs become his own only in the complete degree he mirrors the social unrest of his era. Mars in his house of rebirth makes him the incarnation of his mission, as the Great Commoner, and establishes him as a prime example of the *bucket* temperament.

Abraham Lincoln's case is seen in its most exceptional general lines on page 146. The only appreciable departmental emphasis, other than an elevated moon to account for his public career, is provided by the line of efficiency. A rising Venus gives him an important persistence in the application of his energies to practical problems. It is a quality which can become definite ruthlessness, as in the chart of Joseph Stalin where Venus also is a rising planet, but here it co-operates more constructively with the elevated moon, helping Lincoln perform a real public service. Mars is the leading planet in the *bowl* typing, and this provides a real power of initiative whenever the situation compels action. No matter how the Emancipator may have seemed to vacillate in any superficial view of his career, he was efficient under the indirect emphasis of this one of the four planetary departments. Here the guidance for any astrological interpretation of his life is complete. As in the cases of Andrew Carnegie and Lewis Carroll, the focus of his life does not reach out beyond this first area of group-centered activity.

The chart of Evangeline Adams is interesting, in comparison with Lincoln, because she has a rising Venus, and exhibits its persistent interest in practical everyday ends. In her life, however, the department of efficiency is the least importantly emphasized one of the four. Only this one detail can be added to the summary of focal points on page 147.

The horoscope of Theodore Roosevelt, for which the line of personality affords the most vital guidance, is interesting now as an example of a rising Mars in the cases where the key planets of affairs have no major aspect. The lack of primary emphasis in the line of efficiency indicates his ease of approach to everyday details of life. Yet his initiative is highly sharpened as an unconditioned and naïve impulsiveness, excellently supplementing the even flow of the basic dynamic, and giving a free outlet to the driving necessity seen on page 149.

William McKinley offers a parallel case to Theodore Roosevelt, with a rising Mars and a lack of all other emphases in the department of affairs. The close political association of these men, the latter succeeding the former in the presidency and carrying out his policies for the whole of the given term of office, is an interesting reflection of this parallel. McKinley's unconditioned initiative, under his rising Mars, encourages the ingenuous expression of his personality, described on page 145. Since the fourth department will have no contribution to make in his case, the preliminary analysis of his life ends at this point.

Mars is the elevated planet in the chart of Carl Jung, and gives the Swiss psychologist an important power of initiative, not so much in any expression of his own personality as in a furthering of his life-work and its contribution to the group-welfare. This has been foreshadowed in the summary on page 148, and it is the final point in necessary guidance, since the fourth set of planetary pairs makes no further contribution.

The case of Henry Ford is superficially surprising, because the line of efficiency is without emphasis through any major aspect, and in one sense Henry Ford is the very embodiment of efficiency. However, this is merely another detail of his remarkable freedom from personal considerations, as this has been summarized on page 145. An elevated Venus provides a supplementary emphasis in the department, and gives him his carry-through in practical affairs, or an instinct for the romantic in business, which parallels the service of Mars and its supplementary emphasis on a more direct initiative in Carl Jung's life.

The line of efficiency has a subordinate indication in the life of Edgar Allan Poe, through the place of Mars as the leading planet in his *bowl* typing. He gains a measure of freedom in his general initiative, and this is enhanced because the lack of aspect in this department leaves him without any real touch with the problems or issues of his immediate circumstances. The degree to which he is essentially self-centered in all his experience has been summarized on page 142 f., and the guiding survey of his total pattern is complete at this point.

Oscar Wilde's chart presents a case somewhat similar to Poe, because one of the planets of affairs provides the point of emphasis in his *seesaw* pattern. This Venus focus increases his tendency to go to extremes under the *seesaw* type by providing a carry-through capacity, or what may be ruthlessness almost to the point of sadism, and thus significantly reflects the personality deficiency pointed out on page 145.

There are four horoscopes, among the examples, that are entirely devoid of emphasis in the line of efficiency. The fact has real importance in the final summaries of all these cases, but for the present it is only necessary to identify Cecil Rhodes, Upton Sinclair, Helen Keller and Paul von Hindenburg as those to whom the immediate nature of affairs, in consequence, is never a matter of critical issue, or even appreciable interest.

The charts of Carmen Sylva and Abdul Baha require no further analysis, as has been pointed out on pages 142 and 149 f.

Diamond-Jim Brady offers the one example of a quintile aspect in the department of affairs, but Mars and Venus are not prominent otherwise. The sharp indication of talent on this level of things and their manipulation is a striking clue to the native's remarkable success as a salesman and man about town. This artistry helps in a quite literal sense to direct his prodigality into constructive channels, and encourage the self-discovery indicated by his line of personality on page 147.

Mars and Venus in a Square Aspect

The power of Luther Burbank's horoscope is revealed most tellingly by the subpattern in his department of affairs. The rising Mars identifies the practical dynamic of his career, indicating his unconditioned initiative. The fact that Venus establishes the point of emphasis in his fixed T cross is an indication of his genius for rounding out as well as starting things. The square aspect accentuates the trial and error genius of his *seesaw* typing, and provides the struggle necessary for the employment of his energies. The general trend of his life is summarized on page 145, and the guiding over-view of his potentialities is now complete, since the final line of determination is without emphasis.

The same dynamic aspect, also supplemented by a rising Mars, accentuates the initiative of Stephen Foster, and provides him with a necessity to struggle, thereby creating materials for his composition. This spur to restless activity accentuates his extraordinary talent, analyzed on page 144.

The line of efficiency is emphasized in the horoscope of George Bernard Shaw by Mars as a singleton and a handle planet in his *bucket* typing, as well as by the square of Mars and Venus, which leads him to struggle for the reconstruction of every situation in which he finds himself. The special headstrong initiative of Mars is given some depth of sensitivity, or a desire to be pleasing to others, by the rising Saturn, however, and in general the creative agony of soul, described on page 147 f., overshadows the more superficial manipulation of circumstances because the square of Jupiter and Saturn is considerably stronger than the Mars-Venus relation.

Mars and Venus in a Trine Aspect

The effective degree to which George Gershwin achieves an intimate touch with the life of his day is shown by Mercury's position as the point of emphasis in his common T cross, and by its place as the elevated planet in his horoscope. Mars and Venus, through their trine, give him the same free momentum that has characterized his line of vitality, but the unusual emphasis of mind by his Mercury is an indication of his gift for applying this flow of efficiency on an intellectual level. His easy creative activity contributes to the pattern of a life entirely carried along by the psychological compulsions explained on page 150.

The chart of Leon Trotsky parallels Gershwin's because Mercury, placed at the point of emphasis in a common T cross, also supplements a trine aspect in the line of efficiency. Trotsky's cosmic cross calls for a more fundamental struggle in establishing the basis for his existence, however, and he has a greater integration in practical everyday and social terms. His talent for public service, summarized on page 142, is enhanced in this department by the special understanding of people revealed by his Mercury.

Algernon Swinburne has an elevated Venus, in addition to the trine between the key planets of this department, and this emphasis of the negative planet not only encourages a smoothness of momentum in his superficial affairs, but also indicates the tendency of events to cushion him, to let him drift through life to the very end. His everyday relations are seen through rosy glasses, for better or worse. He is freed from external struggle, so that he can face the task of self-discovery as this has been analyzed on page 147, but there is nothing here to drive him towards achievement. Moreover, there is no further emphasis, in a fourth line of self-determination, to diminish the self-centered focus of this life. Guidance for any interpretation of the chart is complete.

Mars and Venus in a Sextile Aspect

The line of efficiency in the horoscopes of Conan Doyle and Jeff Davis is of special importance because the sextile aspect is also an effective septile, indicating an irrevocable drift in affairs. The inevitability in Jeff Davis' life is definitely foreshadowed on page 145, and through the preceding analysis. Consistently evident in his generally over-fluid pattern, it instruments his particular dramatization of the hobo's career.

Sir Arthur's case is less primitive. He has Mercury as a point of stimulus in his important T cross in fixed signs, and this supplementary emphasis endows him with the practical mental temperament already identified under similar conditions in the charts of George Gershwin and

Leon Trotsky. The septile in everyday affairs, rather than indicating the uncompromising and studied irresponsibility of a Jeff Davis, identifies the persistent self-stimulation of an author's creative temperament. As summarized on page 144, Doyle is not actuated by self-consideration, by conscious motives and designs, but instead is carried along by the very fascination of his own writing.

The horoscope of Karl Marx differs from those of Jeff Davis and Conan Doyle, not only because the sextile functions in its own genius, but because the emphasis on the life as a whole has a much greater pointing. The basic ingenuousness of the self-centering is reviewed on page 150, and the sextile here merely contributes to the correspondingly fluid nature of affairs. However, the rising Mars places the direction of the momentum in the native's own initiative, and makes it more than usually easy for him to establish the momentum according to his own wishes. He did not care to be bothered with things immediately at hand, any more than necessary, and as a result he drew back and let the world become a theater. He used passing events as the substance of his theorizing and let Friedrich Engels take care of his bread and butter. He made the momentum of the world itself the vehicle for his philosophy. Under his rising Mars he started a new momentum, all his own, and under his horoscopic patterning it moved as freely and powerfully as any other.

The chart of William James offers no supplementation for the sextile in this department of affairs, and the fourth line of self-determination presents no emphasis at all, as far as can be known without an exact birthtime. The group-centered side of the native's life is unquestionably subordinate to the creative and self-centered genius summarized on page 140 f. The everyday and easy flow of events contributes a facility to his genuine subjective or philosophical understanding, and rounds out all possible points of guidance for the interpretation of his horoscope.

Section Four

THE LINE OF CULTURE

The fourth planetary department consists of Uranus and Neptune, with Pluto as an additional member. These are the bodies discovered in modern times, a fact which determines their basic meaning. Aspects between them, formed very slowly, define age groups, or the characteristics of certain periods of history rather than strictly personal distinctions among people. Thus, all individuals born in and around 1817-1827 have the conjunction of Uranus and Neptune, which will not occur again until 1987-1998. The opposition is found, among contemporary or near-contemporary charts, only in the 1903-1914 period. There are, of course, two times of sextile, square and trine as against each one of conjunction and opposition, but the same general limitation prevails. The aspects are significant when present in a horoscope, revealing how the native's life or surviving influence is sharpened by the special responsibilities of these particular periods, but the absence of aspect shows not so much a lack of important social relationship as the presence of a certain life-pattern. It identifies individuals who are free from involvement in the various transition activities of modern times. Each planet, when taken by itself in relation to members of other departments, reveals important details of the life-pattern, but as a matter of definite interpretation rather than as any factor in the basic guidance to analysis.

Uranus is the most regular of the new planets, judged by the nature and position of its orbit. Because of this fact, and also because it was the first to be discovered and is the one nearest the earth, it becomes the positive member of the department. It represents the outreach of man into new and larger realms of experience, and identifies the point in the horoscope where the native achieves his "independence", or is able to command the greatest degree of co-operation from life as a whole. It indicates the native's originality at the best, and his eccentricity at the worst.

Neptune has the only orbit with an appreciably irregular placing, according to Bode's empirical law for describing the planetary distances from the sun, and it probably has an exceptional axial movement as well. It was the second of the three new bodies to be discovered, and it moves in the position nearest the earth after Uranus. Because of its deviation from the expected, it indicates a more or less out-of-pattern or even rebellious type of activity. This is the basis for its establishment as the negative planet in the department. It reveals the hidden compulsions or intangible and seemingly perverse factors in world affairs. It indicates an individual's "obligation" to his group, or his ties to his age and race. It is his social instinct at the best, and his unsocial stirrings or blind destructiveness at the worst.

Pluto is found at the proper distance from the sun in the terms of Bode's law, but its orbit is otherwise the most exceptional of the eight true planets known to astronomers and used by astrologers. Both the eccentricity or elongation, and the inclination to the ecliptic or tilt, are much greater than obtains in the case of Mercury, the only other of the eight bodies with marked irregularity in these respects. This fact links Pluto, the most recently discovered planet, with Mercury. Mercury has always ruled mentality, or oblique participation in experience, i.e., the vicarious capacity of the individual. Pluto takes its astrological rôle as an indicator of the cosmic mind, expressing this analogy to Mercury. It reveals the great drifts in racial ideas, the work of conscious or unconscious propaganda, the general behind-the-scenes relations of man's expanded or modern culture. It is a clue, in the individual chart, to the native's broad and largely unsuspected response to developments in human society, and in this reveals his basic "impressionability."

The relation between Uranus and Neptune, measuring the socially-conscious side of self in positive and negative phases of co-operation with the group in a dynamic way, or with the general environment in a static sense, reveals the "line of culture" in any chart. This constitutes the "department of society" and it indicates the group-centered involvement of the individual with his fellows, the subpattern of an organic as in contrast with a practical business of civilization.

Uranus and Neptune in a Conjunction Aspect

The horoscope of Stephen Foster and Karl Marx are the two cases in which the conjunction of the key planets, in this department of society, indicates a significant lack of cultural perspective, or an intensification of some point of important self-immolation within a social momentum. The manner in which Foster's life is held to a point of consistent struggle in the matrix of his general milieu is explained on page 158 f., and the final detail of preliminary analysis in his case is the realization that his creative efforts were exceptionally concentrated at a given moment in a definite cultural development. This might well be to the end that he thereby would become its true interpreter.

Karl Marx is also uniquely the prophet of a very concentrated point of realization in racial history, although according to quite a different pattern. There is the equally complete separation from the immediate concerns and conscious self-evaluations of the group. The practical importance of this social insulation is pointed out on page 161. While Foster caught the living spirit of the American southland, a cultural island in world development, and proceeded to preserve it through his songs, Marx made an isolated retreat for himself in the midst of a toppling phase in Western culture, and thereby created a fresh basis for human experiment and growth. Neptune as the leading planet in the German thinker's *seesaw* patterning made him more aware of his own potential significance than was possible in Foster's case. Moreover, the chart of Marx is exceptional in the fact that all four planetary departments have a sharpened function, due to the presence of a major aspect between their key planets. This is added testimony to the dynamic self-determination making him a prime mover in world-wide social reform, rather than the composer or artist.

Uranus and Neptune in an Opposition Aspect

There is no illustration of this aspect among the twenty-eight examples, but the horoscope of George Washington, which shows a Jupiter-Saturn opposition, has the same planetary emphasis in his line of culture. The native himself revealed no conscious response to the new order in social development, even as far as Uranus indicated and measured the trend, but acted instead on his intuitive sense of the job to be done, as a personal and conscious quickening under the other aspect. Following the discovery of Neptune the country as a whole, to the degree its destiny is indicated in the terms of its founder's surviving influence, became aware of its opportunity as a cultural proving-ground, and only then began to realize that it must take its place as one of the great world powers.

Uranus and Neptune Not in Any Major Aspect

The absence of major aspect in this department of society, in the cases where there is no supplementary emphasis of the three planets, is hardly significant individually, as already suggested, and the horoscopes of eleven out of the twenty-eight examples therefore need no discussion. These are the charts of Abdul Baha, Luther Burbank, Andrew Carnegie, Lewis Carroll, William James, Carl Jung, Abraham Lincoln, William McKinley, Edgar Allan Poe, Algernon Swinburne and Carmen Sylva.

Pluto is significant in the case of Heny Ford because it completes a cosmic cross, of which it is also the point of stimulus. This emphasis of Pluto, when neither Uranus nor Neptune has any pattern-function in the life, implies a type of work which gains its real importance in the light of social potentialities, and is an additional emphasis in the response of Ford to the new potentials of the culture. His genuine detachment from the older compulsions of business and industry has been anticipated on page 156 f.

The horoscope of George Gershwin is exceptional in the fact that Neptune and Pluto together constitute the point of application in his typing. This indicates the emphasis on a particular transition in the cultural development, and parallels the artistic insulation of Stephen Foster. It strengthens the interpretative competency of Gershwin, analyzed on page 159.

The fact that Neptune is rising, and that Uranus is the point of application in his *seesaw* typing, is an indication of cultural significance in the chart of Paul von Hindenburg. He was a striking link between the old monarchy and the new Germany, as well as an instrument in the rise of Nazism, and in all an almost wholly blind agent of events in the sense of the discussion on page 143 f. Uranus gives him a unique capacity for accomplishment, but his retrograde and intercepted Neptune indicates his deep response to developments of little essential concern in his own personal evolution.

The horoscope of Theodore Roosevelt is the only example of either quintile or septile in this department, and also the only one of the twenty-eight charts in which both aspects appear as primary indicators in the four planetary departments. The quintile in his line of culture emphasizes Roosevelt's talent for realizing the real trends in world affairs, and accounts for the consummate skill with which, almost single-handedly, he elevated the United States to the status of a first-class power. Pluto's place as the planet establishing his fixed T cross shows the surviving importance of his contribution to American life. The septile in his line of personality endows him with a driving sense of necessity in his actions, summarized on page 156, and this in turn makes it possible for him to achieve the social significance revealed by the quintile here. He illustrates the conscious performance of great cultural service to the race, in sharp contrast with the blind instrumentality of Hindenburg.

Uranus and Neptune in a Square Aspect

The horoscope of Evangeline Adams is the only illustration of the square aspect in the line of culture. Her necessity for struggle, in this area of social foundations, becomes the vicarious experience or creative and interpretative capacity which she brings to a practical, everyday service as indicated on page 155. Pluto is the point of stimulus in her fixed T cross, showing her surviving influence in the realm of ideas, a prophet of the new or truly modern astrology.

Uranus and Neptune in a Trine Aspect

Of the four horoscopes with this smooth momentum in the department of society, Jeff Davis has Neptune and Pluto rising, and responds to the influence of both in developing the dynamic self-assertiveness of his *bundle* temperament. He and the world co-operate simply and easily in the basic inevitability of his being, as this is seen in recapitulation on page 160.

The charts of Helen Keller and Upton Sinclair are similar to the extent that both of them, under the trine in their line of culture, respond easily to the special needs of the present age. Uranus is an elevated planet in both charts, permitting an independence of self-expression that would have been impossible except in modern times, and neither one has any emphasis in the more superficial department of everyday affairs, so that the social freedom given by Uranus at its best has an exceptional chance to function. The racial momentum provides unusually smooth and fundamental direction for the achievement of these natives, aiding the self-determination which has been summarized in Helen Keller's case on page 145, and in Upton Sinclair's on page 150.

Leon Trotsky's trine in his line of culture equips him for a freely functioning co-operation with events and social trends, and facilitates the tight integration of his life on the immediate side of experience, as this is explained on page 159 f. The position of Pluto, expanding his T cross in common signs to the X form, and giving this X cross a special linking with the important T cross in fixed signs, indicates the surviving and potentially universal value of his martyrdom.

Uranus and Neptune in a Sextile Aspect

The horoscope of Cecil Rhodes is somewhat parallel to those of Helen Keller and Upton Sinclair. Like them, he has no emphasis in the department of affairs. The smooth momentum in his life is provided by a sextile instead of a trine, however, and the special emphasis in his line of culture is by Neptune rather than Uranus. Neptune is the point of stimulus in his important T cross in common signs, and it endows him with the power to give expression to the aspiration of the masses. Added to his strong personal sense of responsibility, described on page 143, this cultural dynamic gives him the feeling of a larger obligation and is an important final confirmation of the power shown by his *locomotive* typing.

The charts of Diamond-Jim Brady, William Jennings Bryan and Oscar Wilde have considerable similarity in the fact that all three lives have been caught up by the typical momentums of modern life, indicated by the sextile in the department of society, and that all have Uranus emphasized by house situation. Uranus is rising in the cases of Brady and Bryan, endowing them with the freedom of social opportunity, together with the particular sensitiveness to new conditions, which complete the guidance to interpretation. Their capacity for unique activity in broad social affairs supplements the analysis brought to a focal point on page 158 for Brady, and on page 154 f. for Bryan.

Uranus is an elevated planet in the case of Oscar Wilde, and this establishes an over-rulership by the line of culture in his public affairs, showing why the circumstances of his life consistently tend to put him into original or eccentric situations. This social direction supplies the final point in guidance for any detailed delineation of his character, rounding out the analysis on page 157.

The horoscope of George Bernard Shaw is emphasized in its exceptional strength of originality in much the same way as the chart of Karl Marx, although Shaw has the productiveness of a sextile and Marx the emphasis of a conjunction in this line of culture. Shaw lacks the supplementary emphasis provided by the position of Neptune as a leading planet in the other case, but he has the momentum of the sextile rather than Marx's lack of perspective in this department. Like the German, however, the Irishman has all four planetary departments represented by a major aspect between the key planets. This is a degree of true self-integration found only in these two examples out of the twenty-eight, and it confirms the unusually dynamic centering of Shaw's life described on page 159.

The final chart emphasized in its line of culture by the easy momentum of the sextile aspect is the case of Conan Doyle, marked also by a lack of supplementary direction in this department of society. As a result there is a tendency for his whole life to move along without any concern over world affairs as such. However, this social drifting aids

Sir Arthur in his keen sensitiveness to the things immediately about him. The lack of interruption to his business of creative authorship is a concluding detail in understanding his exceptional gift of self-stimulation, explained on page 160 f.

Appendix A

THE ASTROLOGICAL ESSENTIALS

The horoscope primarily consists of three factors. The planets are the basis of everything else, and they always indicate "activity". The houses chart the earth's daily motion, and indicate immediate relations or "circumstances". The signs measure the earth's annual motion, and indicate routine relations or "function".

THE TEN PLANETS

☉	Sun	Will	♃	Jupiter	Enthusiasm
☽	Moon	Feeling	♄	Saturn	Sensitiveness
♂	Mars	Initiative	♅	Uranus	Independence
♀	Venus	Appreciation	♆	Neptune	Obligation
☿	Mercury	Mind	♇	Pluto	Impressionability

THE TWELVE HOUSES

First	Angular	Personality
Second	Succedent	Resources, Money
Third	Cadent	Environment, Brethren, Communication, Short trips
Fourth	Angular	Home, End of life, Deeper-link parent
Fifth	Succedent	Self-expression, Speculation, Children
Sixth	Cadent	Servants, Service, Sickness
Seventh	Angular	Partnerships, Competition, Opportunity
Eighth	Succedent	Legacies, Regeneration, Death
Ninth	Cadent	Understanding, Religion, Long journeys
Tenth	Angular	Place in life, Profession, Outer-link parent
Eleventh	Succedent	Friends, Hopes, Objectives
Twelfth	Cadent	Hidden support and limitation

Angular houses indicate the more present relations with immediate circumstances. Succedent houses indicate the more potential relations, or the future. Cadent houses indicate the more established relations, or the past.

THE TWELVE SIGNS

Aries	♈ Ram	Cardinal	Fire	Aspiration
Taurus	♉ Bull	Fixed	Earth	Integration
Gemini	♊ Twins	Common	Air	Vivification
Cancer	♋ Crab	Cardinal	Water	Expansion
Leo	♌ Lion	Fixed	Fire	Assurance
Virgo	♍ Virgin	Common	Earth	Assimilation
Libra	♎ Scales	Cardinal	Air	Equilibrium
Scorpio	♏ Scorpion	Fixed	Water	Creativity
Sagittarius	♐ Archer	Common	Fire	Administration
Capricorn	♑ Goat	Cardinal	Earth	Discrimination
Aquarius	♒ Water-carrier	Fixed	Air	Loyalty
Pisces	♓ Fishes	Common	Water	Appreciation

The four signs established at the equinoxial and solstitial points are cardinal, and show the most direct impact of experience. The four immediately behind are common, and show experience in its greatest concern with people. The four which do not touch the basic points are fixed, and show experience as remote or more concerned with ideas. This distinction is known as quadrature. Each cardinal sign is related to a common and a fixed sign to form a triangle in the zodiac, and this distinction is known as triplicity. The three fire signs stem from the vernal equinox, and show experience centered in personal identity. The three air signs stem from the autumnal equinox. They have a special sympathy with fire, and show experience in its concern over theoretical relations. The three water signs stem from the summer solstice, and show experience in its touch with universality. The three earth signs stem from the winter solstice. They have a special sympathy with water, and show experience in its concern over practical relations.

THE RULERSHIPS OF THE SIGNS

Sun	Leo	Cancer	Moon
Mercury	Virgo	Gemini	Mercury
Venus	Libra	Taurus	Venus
Pluto or Mars	Scorpio	Aries	Mars
Jupiter	Sagittarius	Pisces	Jupiter or Neptune
Saturn	Capricorn	Aquarius	Saturn or Uranus

A house is ruled by the planet which rules the sign on its cusp. A planet, placed in a sign ruled by another planet, is ruled by that planet and this is known as "disposition".

THE MAJOR ASPECTS

Conjunction	0°	Square	90°
Sextile	60°	Trine	120°
Opposition	180°		

OTHER ASPECTS IN COMMON USE

Parallel	0°	Septile	51°26′
Semisextile	30°	Quintile	72°
Semiquintile	36°	Sesquiquadrate	135°
Semisquare	45°	Biquintile	144°
Quincunx	150°		

The orb of an aspect is the distance of separation permitted the planets while in aspect, 17° for the sun, 12°30′ for the moon, and 10° for all others, in the case of major aspects. Minor aspects permit only very small orbs. A house cusp is given an orb of 5°.

When two planets, not in proper aspect to each other, are both aspected by a third, this other may bring them into aspect by "translation of light."

A planet moving, carried or taken towards exactness in aspect is "applying", and its activity is strengthened; in the reverse case it is "separating", and weakened.

THE EXALTATION OF THE PLANETS

Aries	Sun	Leo	Neptune	Sagittarius	Dragon's tail
Taurus	Moon	Virgo	Mercury	Capricorn	Mars
Gemini	Dragon's head	Libra	Saturn	Aquarius	Uranus
Cancer	Jupiter	Scorpio	Pluto	Pisces	Venus

This detail of the "essential dignities" is little used in modern astrology. A planet in a sign opposite one it rules is in its "detriment", and opposite its exaltation is in its "fall".

ADDITIONAL COMMON FACTORS

☊ The dragon's head, a point of general "protection"
☋ The dragon's tail, a point of general "self-undoing"
⊕ The Part of Fortune, a point of general "self-interest"

ADDITIONAL TERMS IN COMMON USE

INTERCEPTION is the situation of a planet in a sign which does not lie on the cusp of any house, diminishing its effectiveness in everyday circumstances.

RETROGRADATION is the situation of a planet given an apparent backward movement in the zodiac by the earth, with a diminished functional influence.

STATIONARY is the situation of a planet as it changes from direct to retrograde, or vice versa; when its influence is greatly strengthened.

MUNDANE ASPECT is the situation of planets, not in orb of aspect, in signs which are sextile, square, trine or opposition to each other.

Appendix B

THE FOCAL DETERMINATORS

Hemisphere Emphasis is the case where all ten planets are situated on one side of the horizon or meridian axis. When all the planets are east, or in the ascending hemisphere, the native is the immediate author of his own destiny. If all are west, or in the descending hemisphere, he must adapt himself to the opportunities he finds. When all are south, or above the earth, he lives objectively or more in public, and when all are north, or below the earth, he lives more subjectively or in private.

Singleton is the case where a single planet occupies a hemisphere, indicating the same emphasis as though all ten were there, but also revealing a strictly limited focus of activity, shown by the nature and place of the planet in question.

Cosmic Cross is the case where two planets in opposition have another one square to both of them, creating the T cross, or where still another one completes a second opposition to the squaring body, giving squares all around in an X cross, or grand cross. Both forms indicate a life emphasized in the terms of quadrature. The T cross is a splendid dynamic; the X cross tends to diffusion.

Grand Trine is the case where two planets in trine to each other are both in trine to a third, and it indicates a life emphasized in the terms of triplicity, with a tendency towards diffusion rather than integration.

Stellium is the case where four or more planets, at least two other than the sun, Mercury and Venus, lie in one house or one sign, indicating a life emphasized in terms of the particular house or sign genius.

Fanhandle is the case where one planet lies in opposition to the principal planet or planets in a stellium, indicating a life with the same great concentration of forces under the stellium, but showing these directed nozzlelike at the opposite side of the wheel. A "miniature fanhandle" is the case where the aggregated planets at one pole of the opposition do not rank as a stellium, but where the other pole supplies the needed supplementation to give the configuration an equivalent focal power.

Singleton in Disposition is the case where one planet alone, resting in a sign it rules, rules all other nine planets, either directly by their place in signs it rules, or indirectly because it rules the planets which in turn rule the others. The special functional emphasis of this one planet indicates a life of great subjective persistence according to its genius.

Preponderance is the case where an unusually large number of planets are found in a given class of sign, such as triplicity or quadrature, or in a particular kind of house, such as angular, succedent or cadent, or where a chart is characterized by an unusual number of some one aspect, indicating a special manifestation of the given emphasis. In the case of triplicity preponderance, the absence of planets in any element is as significant as the presence of a preponderant number, marking a particular need and revealing an active sensitiveness of importance in understanding the life.

Close Pairs is the case in which the planets have a tendency to aggregate in discrete conjunctions, a form of aspect-preponderance which indicates great capacity for a direct attack upon the problems of life.

The Quintile is an aspect which, because of its rarity in the close orb by which alone it can be considered, indicates focal-determinator talent or artistry.

The Septile is an aspect which similarly indicates a fatality or underlying compulsion of focal-determinator importance.

Accidental Dignity is the case where a planet is specially strengthened by its house or aspect situation. When at the midheaven, or nearest one in any group, it is "elevated" and indicates a special emphasis of public position. When just below the horizon, nearest the ascendant, it is the "rising planet", indicating a special emphasis of personality. The many other accidental dignities are little used in modern astrology.

Further Determinators of focal emphasis are either infrequent, or else obvious when encountered. This summary is complete for the needs of the present text, and it is an adequate survey of the technique for all ordinary purposes.

Appendix C

SUPPLEMENTARY HOROSCOPE DATA

All necessary data for the charts is given on pages 180-1 in tabular form. The cusps of six houses are shown, and the other six may be obtained by taking the same degrees, but opposing signs, for each pair of opposite houses. Retrograde planets are indicated by an "R"; stationary planets by a small "s" if they are turning retrograde, and by a large "S" if changing to direct motion.

Name	No.	Type	Name	No.	Type
Beneš, Edouard	1	Bds	Hitler, Adolph	23	Gsp
Besant, Annie	2	Gtq	Hubbard, Elbert	24	Exs
Bismarck, Otto von	3	Ets	Kant, Immanuel	25	At8
Böhme, Jacob	4	Atu	Kipling, Rudyard	26	Ftm
Burton, Richard	5	Ets	Laval, Pierre	27	Bcd
Byron, Lord	6	Ftg	Lenin, Nikolay	28	Es7
Chopin, Frédéric	7	Ddn	Luther, Martin	29	Bcd
Cromwell, Oliver	8	Dht	Morgan, John Pierpont	30	Gte
Dante (Alighieri)	9	Ets	Mussolini, Benito	31	Bcd
Disraeli, Benjamin	10	Dpa	Napoleon (Bonaparte)	32	Etg
Du Maurier, George	11	Esp	Newton, Isaac	33	Ctg
Eddy, Mary Baker G.	12	Cgp	Pasteur, Louis	34	Dce
Ellis, Havelock	13	Ets	Pius XI	35	Ets
Emerson, Ralph Waldo	14	Cts	Robespierre, Maximilien	36	Ggp
Franco, Francisco	15	Ftn	Shakespeare, William	37	Ets
Freud, Sigmund	16	Ets	Shelley, Percy Bysshe	38	F57
Gandhi, Mahatma	17	Ctg	Stalin, Joseph	39	Ets
Goethe, Johann von	18	Ctg	Swedenborg, Emanuel	40	Fxu
Gordon, "Chinese"	19	Egs	Victoria, Queen	41	Dhc
Gould, Jay	20	Gtg	Wagner, Richard	42	Ats
Hamilton, Sir William	21	Esp	Washington, George	43	Ctg
Henry VIII	22	Gt5	Wilson, Woodrow	44	Dht

KEY TO THE TABULATIONS

The numbers, opposite the names above, refer to the tabulated data overleaf. The capital letters, after the numbers, identify the basic typing: A for *splash*, B for *bundle*, C for *locomotive*, D for *bowl*, E for *bucket*, F for *seesaw* and G for *splay*. The small letters give two focal determinators of primary importance, according to the following code:

- **a** angular, succedent or cadent emphasis; preponderance by house position
- **c** concentration of planets in a stellium
- **d** disposition of all planets by one; a singleton in disposition
- **e** elements emphasized by triplicity preponderance
- **f** fanhandle
- **g** grand trine
- **h** hemisphere emphasis
- **m** miniature fanhandle
- **n** no planets in one or more triplicities
- **p** pairing of planets; preponderance of conjunctions
- **q** quadrature preponderance
- **s** singleton planet
- **t** T cross
- **u** unusual emphasis of aspects by preponderance, other than conjunctions
- **x** X cross
- **5** quintile aspect
- **7** septile aspect

	10	11	12	Asc.	2	3	☉	☽	☿
	°	°	°	° ′	°	°	° ′	° ′	° ′
1	♒ 20	♓ 20	♉ 6	23 ♊ 30	♋ 12	♋ 20	7 ♊ 10	22 ♋ 30	22 ♉ 53 R
2	♑ 2	♑ 21	♒ 15	5 ♈ 3	♉ 20	♊ 14	7 ♎ 54	12 ♋ 52	16 ♎ 40
3	♉ 4	♊ 14	♋ 21	19 ♌	♍ 8	♎ 2	11 ♈	9 ♑	17 ♓
4	♑ 5	♑ 23	♒ 20	12 ♈ 45	♉ 25	♊ 17	4 ♐ 26	27 ♉ 50	20 ♐ 52
5	♌ 20	♍ 23	♎ 18	7 ♏ 20	♐ 6	♑ 11	28 ♓	11 ♎	9 ♈ R
6	♒ 20	♈ 2	♉ 19	4 ♋	♋ 19	♌ 8	2 ♒	25 ♋	19 ♑
7	♊ 4	♋ 12	♌ 15	10 ♍ 30	♎ 2	♎ 29	3 ♓ 28	11 ♎ 30	20 ♒ 52 R
8	♑ 8	♑ 21	♒ 16	20 ♈	♊ 6	♊ 24	14 ♉	15 ♍ 30	18 ♉
9	♒ 11	♓ 9	♈ 18	7 ♊	♊ 29	♋ 20	1 ♊	18 ♒	6 ♊ 30
10	♍ 22	♎ 20	♏ 11	28 ♏	♑ 0	♒ 12	20 ♐ 16	27 ♌ 55	12 ♑ 40
11	♐ 12	♑ 0	♑ 19	22 ♒	♈ 18	♉ 21	15 ♓	28 ♑	2 ♈
12	♎ 19	♏ 15	♐ 7	26 ♐ 10	♒ 3	♓ 15	23 ♋ 57	16 ♒ 13	15 ♌ 47 S
13	♐ 17	♑ 4	♑ 24	27 ♒ 30	♈ 26	♉ 26	13 ♒	5 ♒ 30	21 ♑
14	♌ 15	♍ 18	♎ 15	7 ♏	♐ 6	♑ 9	4 ♊	6 ♌	25 ♊
15	♌ 18	♍ 15	♎ 10	9 ♏ 30	♐ 13	♑ 18	12 ♐ 33	14 ♊ 11	28 ♐ 7
16	♈ 4	♉ 13	♊ 24	28 ♋	♌ 16	♍ 7	15 ♉ 56	9 ♊ 30	27 ♉
17	♌ 2	♍ 3	♎ 4	1 ♏ 17	♐ 1	♑ 1	8 ♎ 55	20 ♌ 13	3 ♏ 47
18	♍ 5	♎ 6	♎ 29	17 ♏	♐ 18	♑ 25	5 ♍	12 ♓	29 ♌
19	♑ 0	♑ 18	♒ 13	0 ♈	♉ 17	♊ 11	8 ♒ 19	0 ♉ 57	17 ♑ 6
20	♒ 27	♓ 29	♉ 11	22 ♊	♋ 13	♌ 3	6 ♊	22 ♎	29 ♊
21	♒ 10	♓ 7	♈ 22	18 ♊	♋ 6	♋ 22	11 ♌	0 ♐	0 ♍ 30
22	♊ 26	♌ 5	♍ 4	27 ♍	♎ 17	♏ 16	15 ♋	12 ♈	2 ♌
23	♌ 4	♍ 8	♎ 5	26 ♎ 34	♏ 24	♐ 24	0 ♉ 52	7 ♑ 0	25 ♈ 41
24	♋ 12	♌ 15	♍ 15	10 ♎ 21	♏ 7	♐ 8	28 ♊ 35	14 ♑ 50	1 ♋ 27 R
25	♐ 17	♑ 3	♑ 21	23 ♒	♈ 27	♉ 28	2 ♉	13 ♈ 30	21 ♈
26	♓ 21	♈ 25	♊ 0	0 ♋ 30	♋ 26	♌ 21	9 ♑	15 ♊	24 ♐ R
27	♊ 9	♋ 15	♌ 17	13 ♍	♎ 6	♏ 5	6 ♋ 18	14 ♈ 10	15 ♊ 2
28	♍ 26	♎ 24	♏ 13	28 ♏ 35	♑ 1	♒ 16	2 ♉ 24	3 ♒ 38	12 ♉ 30
29	♈ 14	♉ 23	♋ 4	6 ♌	♌ 23	♍ 15	9 ♏	29 ♌	5 ♏
30	♉ 14	♊ 20	♋ 24	23 ♌	♍ 14	♎ 11	27 ♈ 30	20 ♍ 29	0 ♉ 20
31	♌ 21	♍ 25	♎ 21	11 ♏ 3	♐ 10	♑ 15	5 ♌ 59	8 ♊ 42	5 ♌ 29
32	♋ 20	♌ 24	♍ 23	17 ♎	♏ 14	♐ 16	23 ♌	28 ♑	6 ♌
33	♋ 27	♍ 2	♍ 29	20 ♎	♏ 16	♐ 19	14 ♑	2 ♋	21 ♐
34	♌ 3	♍ 7	♎ 4	26 ♎	♏ 23	♐ 26	5 ♑	18 ♊	1 ♑
35	♈ 9	♉ 17	♊ 26	28 ♋	♌ 17	♍ 10	9 ♊ 37	14 ♍ 56	11 ♊ 17 R
36	♐ 14	♑ 3	♑ 22	24 ♒	♈ 20	♉ 23	15 ♉ 30	28 ♈	5 ♊
37	♉ 26	♋ 9	♌ 12	5 ♍	♍ 26	♎ 20	2 ♉	7 ♉	13 ♈
38	♏ 1	♏ 28	♐ 11	26 ♐	♒ 11	♓ 28	13 ♌	12 ♓	5 ♍
39	♌ 13	♍ 16	♎ 14	6 ♏	♐ 5	♑ 8	28 ♐ 47	4 ♈ 48	9 ♐ 55 S
40	♏ 14	♐ 1	♐ 14	25 ♐	♒ 22	♈ 16	20 ♒	14 ♉	0 ♒
41	♒ 2	♒ 27	♈ 7	6 ♊	♊ 26	♋ 13	2 ♊	4 ♊	9 ♉
42	♑ 29	♒ 23	♈ 2	1 ♊	♊ 23	♋ 11	0 ♊ 30	15 ♒ 30	5 ♉ 34
43	♑ 30	♒ 27	♈ 3	18 ♉ 50	♊ 16	♋ 8	3 ♓ 20	17 ♑ 30	6 ♒ 40
44	♋ 3	♌ 6	♍ 6	2 ♎ 40	♎ 29	♐ 0	7 ♑ 40	0 ♒ 3	17 ♑ 20

	♀	♂	♃	♄	♅	♆	♇
	° ′	°	°	° ′	° ′	° ′	° ′
1	19 ♋ 30	26 ♌ 8	1 ♌ 1	12 ♊ 45	24 ♍ 1 R	21 ♉ 26	1 ♊ 23
2	11 ♎ 4 R	15 ♉ 12 R	18 ♋ 25	7 ♓ 28 R	16 ♈ 37 R	28 ♒ 0 R	26 ♈ 3 R
3	4 ♉	1 ♒	5 ♎ R	10 ♒	7 ♐	21 ♐	21 ♓
4	9 ♑ 53	18 ♎ 39	12 ♌ 30	20 ♐ 23	23 ♑ 5	4 ♋ 30 R	29 ♓
5	12 ♓	14 ♓	4 ♈ 30	14 ♈	3 ♑	3 ♑	28 ♓
6	25 ♒	12 ♋ R	17 ♊ R	28 ♒	28 ♋ R	20 ♎ 30 s	16 ♒
7	28 ♒ 20	2 ♈ 27	23 ♈ 15	14 ♐ 33	14 ♏ 16 s	8 ♐ 56	16 ♓ 20 s
8	29 ♉	9 ♈	15 ♋	11 ♎ R	28 ♈	21 ♌ S	21 ♈
9	2 ♋	21 ♋ 30	27 ♉	20 ♊	1 ♉ 30	6 ♌ 30 S	15 ♏
10	21 ♏ 36	19 ♌ 8 s	25 ♏ 28	15 ♎ 6	12 ♎ 57	26 ♏ 54	10 ♓
11	15 ♓	11 ♒	4 ♉	9 ♎ R	24 ♒	1 ♒	12 ♈
12	8 ♌ 54	12 ♊ 44	28 ♈ 22	26 ♈ 17	0 ♑ 12	1 ♑ 3 R	27 ♓ s
13	28 ♐	1 ♈	11 ♊ 30 R	8 ♌ 30 R	29 ♉ 30 R	23 ♓	5 ♉
14	27 ♈	8 ♌	26 ♍ S	14 ♍ S	8 ♎ S	22 ♏	7 ♓
15	7 ♏ 5	16 ♓ 47	15 ♈ 2 R	10 ♎ 49	8 ♏ 35	9 ♊ 49	8 ♊ 30
16	26 ♈	3 ♎ 24 R	29 ♓ 32	27 ♊ 31	20 ♉ 37	19 ♓ 30	4 ♉ 30
17	16 ♏ 27	18 ♏ 24	20 ♉ 10 R	12 ♐ 22	21 ♋ 46	18 ♈ 27 R	17 ♉ 34 R
18	26 ♍ 30	3 ♑ 30	26 ♓ R	15 ♏	19 ♒ R	24 ♋ 30	0 ♐
19	21 ♓ 21	27 ♉ 22	27 ♓ 16	27 ♍ 41 R	17 ♒ 58	27 ♑ 19	12 ♈ s
20	21 ♋	1 ♉	16 ♋	29 ♎ 30 R	4 ♓	6 ♒ s	15 ♈
21	29 ♌ 45	3 ♎	26 ♏ 30 S	11 ♎ 30	17 ♎ 30	25 ♏ 30 R	11 ♓ R
22	1 ♊	22 ♍	25 ♊	6 ♒ R	22 ♑ R	24 ♐ R	15 ♑
23	16 ♉ 42 R	16 ♉ 23	8 ♑ 15 s	13 ♌ 27 S	19 ♎ 30 R	0 ♊ 52	4 ♊ 41
24	19 ♊ 44	10 ♎ 20	6 ♈ 44	2 ♋ 55	23 ♉ 5	20 ♓ 27 s	5 ♉ 12
25	11 ♊	19 ♋	10 ♒	11 ♑ R	2 ♏ R	28 ♉	0 ♎
26	25 ♐	24 ♐ 30	10 ♑	10 ♏	1 ♋ 30 R	8 ♈	4 ♉ R
27	13 ♊ 39	21 ♉ 24	11 ♋ 35	4 ♊ 21	19 ♍ 40	20 ♉ 14	0 ♊ 28
28	16 ♓ 52	23 ♈ 35	26 ♉ 9	28 ♐ 22 s	18 ♋ 16	19 ♈ 40	17 ♉
29	19 ♎	18 ♎	22 ♎	8 ♏	17 ♐	7 ♐	2 ♐
30	19 ♈ 21	12 ♌ 14	8 ♌ 20 S	15 ♏ 4 R	7 ♓ 17	8 ♒ 4	15 ♈ 30
31	21 ♋ 31	13 ♊ 9	18 ♋ 33	7 ♊ 34	20 ♍ 52	20 ♉ 55	0 ♊ 55
32	7 ♋	12 ♍	15 ♏	26 ♋	11 ♉ 30 s	7 ♍	16 ♑ s
33	27 ♒	7 ♉	14 ♓	20 ♓	15 ♏ 30	1 ♐ 30	4 ♊
34	5 ♑ 30	24 ♑ 30	27 ♉ 30 R	3 ♉ 30 R	7 ♑ 30	5 ♑	0 ♈ R
35	11 ♉ 26 R	11 ♊ 41	3 ♉ 36	12 ♋ 52	26 ♉ 0	22 ♓ 31	6 ♉ 26
36	5 ♈	17 ♌	18 ♐	3 ♓	26 ♓	10 ♌ 30 S	22 ♐
37	0 ♊	0 ♋	29 ♋	29 ♋	7 ♐ R	5 ♊	6 ♓
38	12 ♌	25 ♎	25 ♎	2 ♉	19 ♌	27 ♎ 30	23 ♒
39	12 ♏ 47	13 ♉ 10 S	7 ♓ 13	9 ♈ 3 S	8 ♍ 59 s	9 ♉ 30 R	25 ♉ 44 R
40	3 ♑	28 ♈	15 ♑	24 ♎ R	15 ♉	7 ♓	25 ♋
41	27 ♈	18 ♈	17 ♒	29 ♓	23 ♐ R	28 ♐ R	27 ♓
42	29 ♉ 39	3 ♒ 55	3 ♌ 41	18 ♑ 58 R	25 ♏ 46 R	14 ♐ 34 R	21 ♓
43	29 ♓ 29	23 ♏ 14	8 ♎ 36 R	2 ♈ 47	10 ♐ 6	14 ♊ 42 s	17 ♎ 48
44	15 ♒ 55	16 ♒ 20	1 ♈ 18	10 ♋ 55 R	21 ♉ 28 R	17 ♓ 53	4 ♉ 3

Appendix D

NOTES ON EXAMPLE HOROSCOPES

Whenever possible, the forty-nine horoscopes used for illustrative purposes in this book have been referred to those writers, teachers and research people in the astrological field who have been responsible for putting them into print, or making them available for students generally. This has been for the purpose of verification and the elimination of any errors that have been discovered, and for gaining any information that might add to the record. The nineteen horoscopes of public characters, out of the twenty-one charts used similarly in the companion volume *How to Learn Astrology*, were likewise checked in the same fashion a year ago, and any information gained at that time is incorporated in the following notations. The data for these nineteen horoscopes is included in Appendix C, for the sake of individuals and groups who wish to use the two books together as beginning and advanced text in their study. The four additional charts in Appendix C, added because of references in the present volume, have been subjected to the same standards as the other sixty-eight cases.

The most generally accepted source for the charts of outstanding people remains the Alan Leo manual, published under the title *A Thousand and One Notable Nativities* by L. M. Fowler & Co., London. It represents the first scholarly attempt to collect verified or dependable horoscopes, giving the sources and authority for each one in a way to further research and the continuing validation of data. Thirty-two of the seventy-two example nativities used in this text are from the Alan Leo collection, and reference to his manual, in the notations following, is by the figures *1001*. This is understood to indicate the third and latest edition. There is no need for any repetition of the information in this manual, since those who have access to the English magazines and older books should have equal access to the manual as well. Any items of information appearing here are of interest to the general student, who may not have the opportunity for research in an astrological library.

One chart is taken from the Wemyss collection, and three from a book by Evangeline Adams. Two were obtained directly from magazines published in Europe. These references appear in connection with the given nativities. Two others are solar charts, erected without houses, because no dependable information is available other than the birthday. One more was obtained from an author who requests no special mention. The remaining thirty-one horoscopes have been checked and made available for students by twelve American astrologers of prominence, and while many of the twelve may need no introduction to the average reader, an identifying line might be valuable to the newcomer, and especially to anyone wishing to investigate the astrological field.

ELIZABETH ALDRICH is a leading New York astrologer, writer and teacher, former president of the Astrologers Guild of America, and known to most American students through her mundane work.

ELBERT BENJAMINE is the founder and head of the Church of Light in Los Angeles, formerly the Brotherhood of Light, the largest American organization of astrological students. He is a leader in statistical research, using the resources of his widely spread membership for the collection of cases.

MABEL LESLIE FLEISCHER is a leading New York astrologer, writer and teacher, president of the Astrologers Guild of America at the time this book is published, as well as vice-president and one of the founders of the American Foundation for Metaphysical Arts and Sciences.

MANLY P. HALL is probably America's leading occult philosopher, writer and teacher, author of an immense number of books and pamphlets, contributor to many magazines, and the founder and active head of the Philosophical Research Society in Los Angeles.

RALPH E. KRAUM is a Hollywood bookseller and the country's leading specialist in correcting and verifying the horoscopes of well-known people.

HAROLD FRANCIS MANN is a leading New York astrologer, many years president of the Astrologers Guild of America, and one of the founders of the American Foundation for Metaphysical Arts and Sciences.

ELLEN MCCAFFERY is a prominent New York astrologer, writer and teacher, who has specialized in class instruction, and is widely known through her clever and complete home-study courses.

GEORGE J. MCCORMACK is president of the American Federation of Scientific Astrologers at the time this book is written, and has continued as president of the American Academy of Astrologians for many years. He publishes *Astrotech* in Warren Point, New Jersey.

MARGARET MORRELL is a writer and research worker on the staff of *American Astrology Magazine*, who has come into prominence through her specialized work on vocational astrology, and her effective problem-solving techniques.

DANE RUDHYAR is a composer and author of note, the veteran contributor to *American Astrology Magazine*, and a leading writer on the philosophy of astrology since the Lucis Publishing Company of New York put out his *Astrology of Personality*.

EDWARD A. WAGNER of New York is a leading writer, editor and astrological publisher who conducts one of the very successful astrological features syndicated through the newspapers.

AUGUSTA WILLEY is a New York professional astrologer of talent and modesty, not very well known outside the circles of her own clientele.

ABBREVIATIONS

Only three abbreviations are employed, since other references are infrequent.

1001 *1001 Notable Nativities,* introduced on page 182.
AA *American Astrology Magazine,* published by Paul G. Clancy in New York City and the pioneer popular or newsstand monthly.
NAJ *National Astrological Journal,* an influential publication edited by Edward A. Wagner, and now suspended.

THE STANDARDS ADOPTED

Within reasonable limitations, the charts reproduced in the text have been brought to a uniform standard. The policy has been to maintain the cusps as these are presented by other writers and workers, but to correct the planets, if necessary, according to the best tables available. No such correction has been attempted, however, for the horoscopes of births prior to the nineteenth century. The exact minutes of arc have not been computed for these older charts, and variations of only a few minutes have usually been left without change.

As an aid to the eye in a general text of this sort, latitude and longitude are shown only to even degrees, although in many cases the calculations have taken the minutes into account. The cusps, except the ascendant, are also shown in even degrees only and, more often than otherwise, in the next even degree even though actually closer to the preceding one. This is routine practice for the astrologers who make use of the Sabian or Charubel symbolical degrees. It is necessary to note that since the calculations have often involved a midheaven of uneven degrees, any recalculation of the charts in research must work from the ascendant. Where the ascendant itself was obtained with an even degree rising, no closer calculation was attempted, since there is no widespread agreement on usage in noting or reporting birth times, and no way to know whether the corrections for longitude, and for mean to sidereal time, have been employed. The times themselves as given are frequently rounded, and are presumed to be true local time rather than standard zone, although there is no way to be sure that the one has not been mistaken for the other in an original calculation. The times are presented in even hours, halves or quarters as a usual procedure.

The cusps, therefore, are probably more reliable in general. Because many calculations disregard the proper corrections, small differences of minutes are disregarded in the times inserted in the wheel, and this results in some superficial inconsistencies. Except for the Hindenburg horoscope, all cusps have been checked against Dalton's *Spherical Basis of Astrology,* and again small differences have been disregarded in cases where a competent modern astrologer is consistent in his own way of working. In all cases where the planets have been checked, the basis of correction has been *Raphael's Ephemeris.* Other tabulations have been taken from these tables, except in rather recent years, just as in turn these were derived from older calculations for the earlier part of the century, although subjected to some correction.

The detailed data of birth is not given for charts prior to 1800, since only relatively few readers have access to the proper tables for research work. An effort has been made to provide every essential reference for research, but otherwise to save space.

THE SOURCES OF THE HOROSCOPES

ABDUL BAHA This horoscope was presented by Dane Rudhyar after a careful study of the life in *AA* (v.7, n.10, December, 1939, p.29). He explains in a letter that he selected one of two birth times obtained from a friend who had talked at length with Abdul Baha, and adds, "I think the chart fits excellently. The other, with Gemini rising, does not, to my mind. He was thoroughly Piscean by individual destiny, a consummation of an age and in essence Jupiterian. Mars in the fourth house with its ruler retrograde certainly fits his early exile, and so forth. However, this is just *my* opinion."

ADAMS, EVANGELINE This horoscope was supplied by Ellen McCaffery, who reports, "I remember her saying that she had her chart rectified several times, and some astrologers gave Pisces and some Aquarius, and then one day in going over a lot of odds and ends belonging to her father in an attic, she found his diary with the time 8:30 a. m. mentioned."

BENEŠ, EDOUARD This horoscope was obtained from *L'Astrosophie* (April, 1938). The birth is May 28, 1884, Koslau, Czechoslovakia, at 5:08 a.m.

BESANT, ANNIE This is the corrected horoscope from *1001* (p.125). The birth is October 1, 1847, London, at 5:29 p.m.

BISMARCK, OTTO VON This is nativity 254 in *1001*. The birth is April 1, 1815, Schönhausen, at 1:30 p.m.

BÖHME, JACOB This horoscope was published by Manly P. Hall in *NAJ* (v.6, n.8, August, 1934, p.12). Mr. Hall reports that the chart is entirely speculative. "Even the date of his birth has not been officially recorded. My data was accumulated from early editions of his work, and biographical outlines by early authors. The planetary positions are worked out from the ephemeris of his year which I happen to have." The position of Pluto has been added for the date adopted, November 17, 1575 (old style).

BRADY, DIAMOND-JIM This horoscope was published by Miss Laurie Pratt in *AA* (v.3, n.4, June, 1935, p.15). Miss Pratt has verified the chart and gives her authority as the Parker Morrell biography.

BRYAN, WILLIAM JENNINGS This horoscope is from the files of Ralph Kraum, and the data from the *Star of the Magi*, (v.2, November, 1900, p.14). Professor Cunningham wrote to Dr. Hill, attending physician at the birth of Mr. Bryan, who gave the time of birth as "a little after nine in the morning; about 9:15." The chart is rectified to 9:04 a.m., local mean time.

BURBANK, LUTHER This horoscope was provided by Elbert Benjamine, who reports that the data "was given personally to one of our students."

BURTON, RICHARD This is nativity 356 in *1001*. The birth is March 19, 1821, Hertfordshire, at 9:45 p.m.

BYRON, LORD This is nativity 752 in *1001*. The birth is January 22, 1799.

CARNEGIE, ANDREW This horoscope is supplied by Mabel Leslie Fleischer, who reports that "Evangeline Adams got this data from Mr. Carnegie, or someone close to him."

CARROLL, LEWIS This is nativity 125 in *1001*.

CHOPIN, FRÉDÉRIC This is nativity 389 in *1001*. The birth is February 22, 1810, Zelazowa-wola, near Warsaw, at 4:00 p.m.

CROMWELL, OLIVER This is nativity 613 (Gadbury) in *1001*, not 68 (Partridge). The birth is April 26, 1599.

DANTE, (ALIGHIERI) This is nativity 844 in *1001*. The birth is only sure as the "the middle of May", 1265.

DAVIS, JEFF This horoscope was presented by Elbert Benjamine in *World Astrology* (v.3, n.1, January, 1939, p.35). He reports that the data was obtained personally from the "king of the hobos" when he visited Los Angeles.

DISRAELI, BENJAMIN (Lord Beaconsfield) This is nativity 737 in *1001*. The birth is December 21, 1804, London, at 5:32 a.m.

DOYLE, SIR ARTHUR CONAN This horoscope is from the files of Ralph E. Kraum, and was obtained originally from the *Wheel of Life*, (v.3, p.7).

DU MAURIER, GEORGE This is nativity 81 in *1001*. The birth is March 6, 1834, Paris, at 5:45 a.m.

EDDY, MARY BAKER G. This chart is supplied by Mabel Leslie Fleischer, who reports that Evangeline Adams "dug up the information years ago when she lived in New Hampshire, and checked on it for many years, noting events, difficulties with legal matters, death, and so forth." The birth is July 16, 1821, Bow, near Concord, New Hampshire, at 5:33 p.m.

ELLIS, HAVELOCK This is nativity 766 in *1001*. The birth is February 2, 1859, Croydon, Surrey, at 8:15 a.m.

EMERSON, RALPH WALDO This horoscope is from *Astrology, Your Place Among the Stars*, by Evangeline Adams, New York, Dodd Mead, 1934. The birth is May 25, 1803, Boston, at 5:00 p.m.

FORD, HENRY This is the horoscope published by Edward A. Wagner, in the *NAJ* (v.5, n.10, October, 1933) under his pen name, Karl Van Dyke. He writes, "The Ford chart is certainly correct. We obtained the date from an authorized version of his life."

FOSTER, STEPHEN The date for this horoscope was published by Ralph Kraum in his column "Who's Who in the Zodiac", *NAJ* (May, 1935, p.7).

FRANCO, FRANCISCO This horoscope is taken from *Modern Astrology* (May-June, 1937, p.93). The birth is December 4, 1892, El Ferral, Spain, at 4:30 a.m.

FREUD, SIGMUND This horoscope is provided by Mabel Leslie Fleischer, and was printed in *AA* by Dane Rudhyar (August, 1937, p.22). The birth is May 6, 1856, Freiberg, at 9:17 a.m.

GANDHI, MAHATMA This horoscope was obtained from George McCormack. The birth is October 2, 1869, Gujarat, India, at 7:33 a.m.

GERSHWIN, GEORGE This horoscope is from Augusta Willey, who has verified the data for publication.

GOETHE, JOHANN VON This is nativity 640 in 1001. The birth is August 29, 1749.

GORDON, "CHINESE" This is nativity 957 in *1001*. The birth is January 28, 1833, London, at 9:30 a.m.

GOULD, JAY This is nativity 259 in *1001*. The birth is May 27, 1836, Roxbury, Delaware County, New York, at 5:35 a.m.

HAMILTON, SIR WILLIAM ROWAN This is nativity 409 in *1001*. The birth is August 4, 1805, Dublin, at 11:55 p.m.

HENRY VIII This is nativity 494 (Gadbury) in *1001*. The birth is June 28, 1491.

HINDENBURG, PAUL VON This horoscope, published by Manly P. Hall in the *NAJ* (v.5, n.5, p.5) differs from every other chart in the book or appendices because it employs a house-division at variance with ordinary American practice. No alteration has been made in the cusps, although the planetary positions have been checked. Mr. Hall reports that "the Hindenburg horoscope is from a collection of nativities published in Germany and is the chart used by all German astrologers."

HITLER, ADOLPH This chart was published by Manly P. Hall in the *NAJ* (v.5, n.5, May, 1933, p.4). The birth is April 20, 1889, Braunau, Austria, at 6:30 p.m.

HUBBARD, ELBERT This horoscope is from *Astrology, Your Place Among the Stars*, by Evangeline Adams, New York, Dodd Mead, 1934. It is the corrected chart which appears only in the later printings of the book. The birth is June 19, 1856, Bloomington, Illinois, at 1:03 p.m.

JAMES, WILLIAM This is not a complete horoscope. The hour of birth is unknown and it is the "solar chart" used in *AA* and other magazines. The sun's sign and degree are placed on the ascendant, and the other signs with the same degree placed around on the other house cusps. It is important to distinguish between this approximation and the genuine chart, since they look much the same at a first glance.

Jung, Carl This horoscope is based on data obtained by Mabel Leslie Fleischer directly from Dr. Jung himself, and this is the wheel corrected over the prior chart published on the basis of the same data, but with wrong cusps.

Kant, Immanuel This is the corrected nativity from *1001* (p.129). The birth is April 22, 1724.

Keller, Helen This is horoscope 45 in Wemyss' *Famous Nativities.*

Kipling, Rudyard This is nativity 990 in *1001*. The birth is December 30, 1865, Bombay, at 4:50 a.m.

Laval, Pierre This horoscope was published by Harold Francis Mann in *Wynn's Astrology Magazine* (v.7, n.3, July, 1936, p.17), and has been verified by Dr. Mann. The birth is June 28, 1883, Chateldon, near Vichy, at 10:00 a.m.

Lenin, Nikolay This horoscope was published by Dane Rudhyar in *AA* (June, 1938, p.15). The birth is April 22, 1870, Ulyanovsk (Simbirsk), at 9:42 p.m.

Lincoln, Abraham This is the carefully reconstructed horoscope published by Manly P. Hall in the *NAJ* (v.6, n.2, February, 1934, p.12), quite at variance with the more familiar chart erected by L. D. Broughton some seventy years ago. Mr. Hall writes, "I did extensive research at the Chicago Historical Society, and you can depend on the chart as being correct to within a few minutes."

Luther, Martin This is nativity 486 (Cardan) in *1001*. The birth is October 22, 1483, accepted also by Junctinus.

Marx, Karl This horoscope was published by Dane Rudhyar in *AA* (v.6, n.3, May, 1938, p.15), and was the product of his careful research.

Morgan, John Pierpont This is nativity 886 in *1001*. The birth is April 17, 1837, Hartford, Connecticut, at 1:03 p.m.

Mussolini, Benito This horoscope was rectified by Dane Rudhyar, who writes, "This hour seems to me much truer than the usually accepted one." The birth is July 29, 1883, Varano di Costa, Italy, at 1:08 p.m.

McKinley, William This is the corrected horoscope supplied by George McCormack, and it shows considerable variance from the older Broughton chart in common circulation. Mr. McCormack reports that the correction was made by Professor Cunningham in the *Star of the Magi* "about 1900," and that Cunningham got his data from President McKinley's mother.

Napoleon (Bonaparte) This is nativity 731 in *1001*. The birth is August 15th, 1769.

Newton, Isaac This is nativity 739 in *1001*. The birth is January 4, 1643 (new style).

Pasteur, Louis This is nativity 950 in *1001*. The birth is December 27, 1822, Dôle, France, at 2:00 a.m.

PIUS XI (ACHILLE RATTI) This horoscope was obtained from Margaret Morrell. The birth is May 3, 1857, Desio, Milano, Italy, at 8:00 a.m.

POE, EDGAR ALLAN The hour of birth is unknown and this is the "solar chart" explained in the notation under William James. Manly Hall has a true horoscope of Poe in his files with a midheaven at Sagittarius 1° and an ascendant at Aquarius 8°, but the evidence seems insufficient to justify the use of these cusps.

RHODES, CECIL This is nativity 318 in *1001*.

ROBESPIERRE, MAXIMILIEN DE This is nativity 759 in *1001*. The birth is May 6, 1759.

ROOSEVELT, THEODORE This horoscope is supplied by George J. McCormack, who reports that Roosevelt was interested in astrology, at least to the point of himself supplying the time of his birth.

SHAKESPEARE, WILLIAM This is nativity 67 in *1001*. The birth is April 23, 1564 (new style).

SHAW, GEORGE BERNARD This horoscope is the corrected one in *1001* (p. 129).

SHELLEY, PERCY BYSSHE This is nativity 73 in *1001*. The birth is August 4, 1792.

SINCLAIR, UPTON This horoscope was published by Wesley D. Jamieson in *NAJ* (May, 1934, p. 6). Mr. Wagner, editor of the journal, has lost track of the author, as has Ralph Kraum, who supplied him with much of his data. There has been considerable controversy over this birth-hour. Mr. Wagner reports that when Sinclair ran for the governorship in California, "those who put forward the other chart predicted his election and upbraided us for taking a contrary stand. We have always felt the outcome justified both the chart and our judgment. The only inaccuracy known to me and the one which threw everyone off at the time was the date of Merriam, who won the election. The old fox had given out a date, making himself ten years younger than he really was with an eye to overcoming the attack of his opponents based upon the age question."

STALIN, JOSEPH This horoscope was published by Dane Rudhyar in *AA* (July, 1938). The birth is December 21, 1879, Gori, Georgia, at 3:05 a.m.

SWEDENBORG, EMANUEL This is nativity 23 in *1001*. The birth is January 29, 1688.

SWINBURNE, ALGERNON CHARLES This is nativity 968 in *1001*.

SYLVA, CARMEN (ELIZABETH OF RUMANIA) This horoscope is supplied by Elizabeth Aldrich, who has checked it in connection with her mundane work. It was originally printed in *Modern Astrology* (v. 7, new series, 1910, p. 306).

TROTSKY, LEON This horoscope was published by Dane Rudhyar in *AA* (v.6 n.5, July, 1938, p.9).

VICTORIA, QUEEN This is nativity 50 in *1001*. The birth is May 25, 1819, London, at 4:15 a.m.

WAGNER, RICHARD This is nativity 888 in *1001*. The birth is May 22, 1813, Leipzig, at 4:00 a.m.

WASHINGTON, GEORGE This is a corrected horoscope supplied by Ellen McCaffery, who has done considerable research on the nativity, and had the planetary positions checked by Ralph Kraum. The birth is February 22, 1732.

WILDE, OSCAR This horoscope was obtained from Mabel Leslie Fleischer, who says, "Oscar Wilde's year seems to be 1856, which checks with the life in every way, psychologically and in the events, much better than the 1854 date, which is also given." Vivian E. Robson, in his new book *Astrology and Sex* (Philadelphia, David McKay, 1941) takes the 1854 chart from *1001*, and reports, "The particulars originally obtained by an astrologer after the trial were somewhat vague, and were to the effect that birth took place in London at 3:00 a.m. on October 15th of either 1854 or 1856. The astrologer chose the 1854 date as affording a horoscope that better fitted the events, and he presumably rectified the time and corrected the information as to the birth-place which was Dublin and not London. Wilde's biographers, notably Arthur Ransome and R. Thurston Hopkins, give October 16th, 1854 as the date of birth, but in the *Encyclopaedia Britannica* and other modern reference books, it is given as October 15, 1856, which differs not only in the year but in the date also. I have not been able to discover the reason for this change."

WILSON, WOODROW This horoscope is from *Astrology, Your Place Among the Stars* by Evangeline Adams, New York, Dodd Mead, 1934. It is the corrected chart which appears only in the later printings of the book. The birth is December 28, 1856, Staunton, Virginia, at 11:45 p.m.

INDEX

THE HOROSCOPES

POINTS IN CLASSIFICATION

POINTS IN FOCAL DETERMINATION

POINTS IN DELINEATION

GENERAL REFERENCES AND EXPLANATIONS

OTHER IMPORTANT NEW AGE BOOKS

ART AS A GUIDE TO SELF-REALIZATION—*J. Donald Walters*

Art as a Guide to Self-Realization offers a blueprint for the future of art, and shows how art can be a powerful influence for meaningful existence and positive attitudes in society. The book presents a new approach to the arts, one that views both artistic expression and artistic appreciation as creative communication.

ISBN: 81-7822-028-8

THE BOOK OF CHAKRA HEALING—*Liz Simpson*

The Book of Chakra Healing is a comprehensive guide to the ancient Indian system of chakras. These centres of "spinning energy" in the body help to maintain your physical, mental, emotional, and spiritual balance. This book offers practical way to work on your chakras and shows you how to unblock and rebalance your energy. This book will be of great benefit to both health care professionals and lay people and will inspire many to explore and develop their relationship with an integral part of their being—the chakras.

ISBN: 81-7822-043-1

CHAKRA ENERGY MASSAGE—*Marianne Uhl*

This book guides you into the fascinating world of the energy body. Drawing on the knowledge gained by Foot Reflexology Massage, it introduces you to the Chakra Energy Massage. By means of the fine energy channels connecting them to the body's organs and energy centres, our feet reflect our physical and psychic condition. It enables you to acquire basic knowledge needed for Foot Reflexology Massage and Chakra Energy Massage.

ISBN: 81-7822-004-0

THE HEALING HANDBOOK (A Spiritual Guide to Healing Yourself and Others)—*Tara Ward*

In this book the author presents a range of techniques and tools for healing yourself and other, including children and animals. The book features: Techniques for chakra awareness, relaxation, self-assessment, releasing anger and resentment, healing physical conditions, creating a healing sanctuary, increasing sensitivity, developing intuition, protecting yourself, absent healing and provides information about healing tools such as pendulums, crystals, colour, sound, massage, spirit guides.

ISBN: 81-7822-034-2

HEALING THE FUTURE (The Journey Within)—*Deepak Kashyap*

The greatest possibilities of body-cure, says the author, lie in forgetting the body. To the extent we lose body-consciousness and identify with the Spirit, physical disability and mental trauma disappearing on their own. *Healing the Future* is then, an attempted tip-off on the little secrets of holistic living that can be mastered in easy, small steps. This book urges you to treat consciousness as a canvas, and begin adding new colour, shine and texture to your tomorrow from this very instant.

ISBN: 81-7822-039-3